Toxic boss blues

STEVE NEAL

First Printing

Author ~ Steven R. Neal

Cover design ~ Shari Hindman

Graphic design ~ Dianne C. Dementi

Publisher ~ Dementi Milestone Publishing, Inc.
Manakin-Sabot, VA 23103
www.dementimilestonepublishing.com

Cataloging-in-publication data for this book is available from The Library of Congress.

ISBN: 978-0-9898812-7-2

Printed in the USA

Praise for
Toxic Boss Blues: the Enemy of Leadership and Morale

Written with the candor of a street cop and the perspectives of a seasoned police executive, Toxic Boss Blues is a must read for entry level officers through senior managers. Just labeling, describing, and helping us identify the different types of toxic boss behaviors would have been valuable. Yet, Steve takes it further by providing insightful survival tactics and tenets of principled-centered leadership. The scenarios throughout the text bring a sense of context and reality to these important concepts. With 30 years at the local and federal level in this noble profession, I've yet to read a more honest, candid, and spot-on book delving into the devastating consequences of poor leadership and the inspiring results of great leadership.

Jeff Green, PhD
Author: *Decision Point: Real-Life Ethical Dilemmas in Law Enforcement*

Steve Neal's book, *Toxic Boss Blues* is an excellent book and a topic that is in the forefront of every law enforcement officer's mind. How do we go to work every day, in a very demanding and hazardous environment, and then survive the unnecessary stress of poor supervisors and managers who make our daily job exceedingly difficult, unpleasant, and unsafe? This book actually applies to many other career fields and working environments, but especially those which are inherently dangerous and traumatic by the very nature of the job. If you are a police, correctional or probation officer, or even a firefighter, military member, or first responder, you will want to read this book. This book is thought provoking and will benefit those who seek to be true leaders; and, will hopefully fall in the hands of those who need to reflect on their shortcomings. Effective leadership and morale ensures mission success and survivability for today's warrior; and, consequently the very public we seek to protect and serve. Buy this book for yourself. Pass it along to your supervisors.

Leon Ives
GBP Consulting, Investigative and Security Services, Inc.
Author: *Vanished! How to Protect Yourself and Your Children*

Steve Neal is right on the money with his new book *Toxic Boss Blues*. During my career and coming up through the ranks, I also encountered quite a few toxic supervisors. This book is absolutely a must read for anyone wanting to advance through the ranks!

Ray Baxley
Chief of Police at Town of Blountsville
Blountsville, Alabama

Timely, important topic; *Toxic Boss Blues* is a must-read for anyone managing others, as well as anyone dealing with a difficult supervisor! Steve Neal compellingly makes the case for why toxic leaders exist, and gives practical advice for how to navigate through and around the toxic leaders that most of us encounter at some point in our careers. Although the real-life examples are sobering to those who have experienced things all too similar, the advice for maneuvering through the situation is life-altering. What sets this book apart: the DNA core competencies for Principled Leaders and the instructions for how to stand strong and make a difference; "*If you're right, you fight!*"

Joye N. Hearn
Founder, Lead Consultant, and Head Coach at CoachTNT

Toxic Boss Blues should be a wake-up call to the administrations of all police and related Para-military organizations. Nothing destroys the morale of public servants more than poor or toxic leadership. In nearly every leadership class I attended during my career, officers and mid-level supervisors from across the country complain about their administrations far more so than the daily challenges of law enforcement. While certainly some officers may need to be disciplined or even terminated, too many of the truly good ones often leave for other jobs or other agencies due to hostile or inconsistent leadership. Toxic leaders aren't alone in their departments; someone of higher or equal rank agrees with them and allows them to do what they do. Bad leadership is mostly a learned behavior. *Toxic Boss Blues* will benefit everyone in the organization and chain of command - *READ IT!*

Jim Herring
Chief Warrant Officer, U.S. Army Special Forces, North
Carolina Army National Guard
Silver Star Medal recipient by all United States Armed Forces
Retired Police Lieutenant

DEDICATION

This book is dedicated to all, past and present, who commit themselves to serving as the guardians of homeland security.

Law enforcement, military, firefighters, and other protection industries are our true heroes. The men and women warriors of public service organizations willingly lead the fight for peace and freedom at home and abroad. Our gladiators keep us safe, while living the principles of duty, sacrifice, and valor. I humbly offer my gratitude and respect to all who have served honorably.

Toxic Boss Blues is also dedicated to Franklin D. Neal, my father, who to this day is still the greatest person that I have ever known. A man of iron will and uncompromising principles, dad taught me to work hard, make good decisions and to solve problems successfully by using the golden rule. I will never be able to repay him, a master of diplomacy and tact, for teaching me how to be a man.

Acknowledgements

A special appreciation is extended to mi amigo and mentor, Dr. Dick Leatherman. I value the many hours of advice, consultation, and good ole fashioned friendship that we have shared the last couple of decades. Your example, advocacy, and encouragement provided much of the motivation that has guided me through this project. I hope that one day I will learn to be as good a friend to you as you have been to me. Go Spiders!

Thank you to the many public safety professionals who offered wisdom, counsel, and real-life experiences that enhanced the quality of this book. It has been my good fortune and a pleasure to serve the community beside some of the most remarkable people on the planet. It would not have been possible to prepare an authentic toxic supervisor text without the special contributions of peers, co-workers, colleagues, and friends from around the country.

Most importantly, I ask my family, and extended family, to accept my heartfelt thanks for the love and support you have shown to me through the years. Each of you are embedded deep in my soul, and I will always hold you close. My wish is that you experience success, happiness, and peace throughout your lifetime.

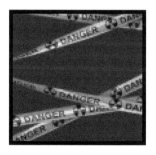

FOREWORD

BY PATRICK YOES

From their first day on the job, law enforcement officers are taught that they are to take control of every situation, without exception. After all, their life, or someone else's may very well depend upon it.

However, when it comes to leadership above them within their organization, they often feel powerless. They go from controller of every situation to being controlled.

How they are able to adapt to this internal conflict will define their entire career.

By its very nature, public safety creates an environment where stringent rules and regulations must be enacted to maintain public trust for law and order. Seeking balance in this often difficult and widely subjective equation is no easy task. Public safety officers must contemplate many challenges on almost a daily basis and thus, the lessons of leadership are learned through trial and error and by the influence of peers within the organization.

Ask any public safety employee how they became interested in this noble profession and their answers will likely be the same. It was not a slick colorful advertisement in a magazine nor was it a newspaper job posting. It was not action filled television commercials or loud radio spots. It was because someone within this profession recruited them. Perhaps it was a family member, friend, or a school resource officer that recognized their positive qualities and guided them down the public service path.

Each entered the academy with a mixture of both excitement and apprehension served up in equal portions. They are excited about being part of something far greater than themselves and at the same time wonder if they have what it takes to meet the expectations of their peers. Months later, they emerge from the classroom in a freshly pressed uniform, polished leather gear and a weapon strapped to their side, ready to change the world with their newly found knowledge.

That is when their true education begins. It is not the academy that has taught them to be a cop; there, they only learned the basics.

Much as they were recruited, it will be a peer, seasoned veterans within their organization, who will guide them down the public safety path.

Leadership learning is no different, it doesn't necessarily happen through a training course or reading books; rather, it is a mixture of education and life's experiences to help form an ever-changing philosophy that will grow with every experience.

Young recruits are overwhelmed trying to understand a new job and all the challenges it brought with it. Rapid change and constant transition created many emotional dynamics for a new impressionable officer to deal with. Uncertainty can trigger all kinds of behavioral and emotional reactions from leaders and their reports that are affected by the decisions made by other higher in their governing hierarchy. Understanding the conflict process within us can help mitigate this difficult journey.

Each officer will have several mentors during their career, likely in their chain of command, each of whom will impart their years of practical experience to develop and hone their cop and survival instincts. These leaders will serve as a "real-world reality-based consoler. Each mentor's leadership traits will factor greatly in that new officer's development and effectiveness.

Unfortunately, not every leadership trait or style learned will be desirable or effective. Learning these lessons can vary from one extreme to another as my assigned training officers each possessed a different style of mentoring. Some inspired me to be more, others not so much. From positive and empowering leaders to habitually negative nay-sayers, each played a role in my career development.

It can be argued that a new officer's success and longevity can be measured by the traits of the leaders above them. Steve Neal's *Toxic Boss Blues* contrasts a wide range of leadership styles and helps the reader consciously evaluate each style. His thought-provoking style guides readers through a logical analysis that exposes toxic consequences of inconsistent and inept leadership.

Whether you are a new recruit or a seasoned veteran, *Toxic Boss Blues* has something for you. For the new impressionable officer, Steve illustrates the many pitfalls in their path and offers tips to safely navigate beyond them. For the seasoned veteran, it offers an objective lesson of self-reflection. For both, Steve helps them to become the progressive leader they are capable of being.

As you read each chapter, ask yourself which of these leadership traits that you feel your peers would say best describes you. For the young officer, ask yourself what leadership style would you strive to adopt as your own? *Toxic Boss Blues* can be a valuable tool in achieving your leadership goals. That is, if you are objective and humble enough to do so.

Patrick Yoes
National Secretary, Fraternal Order of Police
Author: *Chest Deep and Rising – The Hurricane Katrina Nightmare*

PREFACE

Sadly, toxic bosses are found everywhere. Though the illustrations and stories in this book come from the world of law enforcement, there is no doubt that the behaviors and actions described in *Toxic Boss Blues* easily transcend every industry. I strongly suspect that many in the armed forces, fire service, government, or paramilitary sectors will relate to and empathize with the targets of abuse and the tawdry relationships chronicled within the confines of the following chapters.

The leadership and oversight of those working in rigid hierarchal organizations is at best an inexact science. It is imperative that the reader does not mistake the positive management concepts found in *Toxic Boss Blues* with supervisory weakness. Respectful and artistic leadership should not be misconstrued as lowering standards, kinder and gentler policing, blue ribbons for all participants, political correctness, or the wussification of law enforcement.

Discipline, authority, and command are essential elements of every strong and effective work environment. Excellent leaders do not coddle or tolerate poor performance. If teaching, training, guidance, and tutelage fail to develop an employee, then stakeholder integrity dictates that the worker must be properly separated from the workforce. Professionals know how to coach, mentor, correct deficiencies, and enforce standards of success without being rude, hostile jerks.

Mean spirited, malicious, discourteous, discriminatory, or deliberately hurtful behavior towards law enforcement officers by their bosses should never be acceptable. The "contempt of cops" by those in the chain of command creates toxic boss blues. Poisonous bosses who devalue, denigrate, chastise, and humiliate in the name of discipline and learning are operating from a platform of ignorant aggression.

Great leaders combine dignity and decency with order, prerogative, and governance. The best amongst us understand that treating other people as if they matter encourages constructive relationships that pay huge dividends in the workplace. Civility, tact, and gracefulness are sophisticated leadership skills that facilitate greater employee pride, self-respect, purpose in our work, and enhancement of our product.

Toxic Boss Blues

The Enemy of Leadership and Morale

Table of Contents

Chapter 1

INTRODUCTION

Law enforcement is one of the most noble and awe-inspiring professions in the world. Nearly all peace officers join the family of public safety because they hold honorable and principled belief systems close to their hearts. Our brothers and sisters demonstrate enormous integrity, are filled with compassion, and truly serve the needs of others every single day. Public safety officers willingly put themselves in harm's way and live the biblical quote "Greater love hath no man than this, one lay down his life for his friends." Law enforcement brethren keep the peace and ensure the security of the homeland.

Not everyone has what it takes to meet the demanding requirements of the law enforcement profession. Many agree that there are numerous values, beliefs, and behaviors that are commonly shared by a majority of successful law enforcement officers. One of the great contradictions of public safety is that some of the same traits and characteristics needed for extraordinary achievement, if applied conversely or taken to the extreme, cause tremendous stress and pain for the guardians of our domestic freedoms.

The culture of a workplace is often shown by its principles, beliefs and what is considered accepted behavior. Good leaders question, probe, assess, validate, and challenge on a regular basis. When the culture is positive, it encourages individuals to adopt appropriate activities that promote respect of others. In contrast, the toxic leader often creates an atmosphere of negativity and dissention, as opposed to inspiration and camaraderie. While obvious even to a casual observer, toxic managers hamper creativity, depress learning, frustrate conversations, and impede innovations.

In law enforcement circles, it is often said that threats from the street are potentially lethal, but that the *threat from the enemy within* is a far worse hazard to a law officer's health and well-being. When nastiness is allowed to flourish in a toxic management culture; confidence, assertiveness, decisiveness, teamwork, and values-based supervision can transform into vicious bullying, untruthfulness, arrogance, indecisiveness, immorality, micromanagement, revenge, and retribution. The evil of toxicity and negative behavior exposes our peace-keeping warriors to unnecessary and potentially life threatening dilemmas.

Abraham Lincoln once said, "Nearly all men can stand adversity, but if you want to test a man's character, give him power." Few vocations on earth adorn its practitioners with the vast authority granted to civilian police officers. Because they cause such dreadful harm to a remarkable occupation, our journey will focus on the toxic few who fail Lincoln's test of character.

Ladies and gentlemen, management toxicity, a plague denied by many in leadership positions, is the elephant in the room for public safety. Practitioners know that the problem is real, and that its impact is poisonous. A large percentage of officers feel far more stress from their own supervision, than they do from simply doing their job. More than a few officers believe they have been victimized by those who are in charge at their own workplace.

Another way of looking at the oddly paradoxical problem of public safety toxicity is through the lens of excessive force. The application of excessive, unnecessary, or improper use of force against the public is rightly one of law enforcements pivotal issues. Yet, far too many officers are experiencing unnecessary, unreasonable, and repugnant psychological force heaped upon them by their own bosses. Why are toxic bosses allowed to get away with applying indecent prerogative to their organization's most valuable assets?

Agencies with high turnover and low morale have a plethora of incompetent toxic authority figures. The most valuable weapons against management tyranny; knowledge, courage, and righteousness, will help to marginalize the enemy within and mitigate the toxicity. Those best able to accurately identify the toxic threats, understand their impact, and implement effective survival techniques are those most likely to persevere and prosper.

I have enormous respect for all in law enforcement who serve admirably. Performing principled work in the streets is an astoundingly honorable endeavor. The goal of *Toxic Boss Blues* is to keep law enforcement employees healthy by identifying and neutralizing the deadly management viruses that combine to form the killer from within.

How to Survive the Threat from the Enemy Within

Chapter 2

WHY ARE TOXIC AUTHORITY FIGURES PERMEATING LAW ENFORCEMENT

Let's lay the cards on the table and speak the truth, the whole truth, and nothing but the truth. Almost everyone associated with law enforcement knows that there are too many supervisors and managers (many at or near the top of the profession) who are toxic—they are discourteous, noxious bullies. As I prepared the text of this book, law enforcement officers from around the world shared stories of disturbing abuses at the hands of their toxic bosses. It may be helpful if we examine some of the influences and circumstances that place law enforcement at an unusually high risk for toxic leaders.

Nature of the Business

To serve and protect is front and center with nearly every law enforcement agency in the world. Law enforcement is, and hopefully always will be, predominantly a service industry that requires a caring mindset. The primary motivation of most officers is a heartfelt desire to interact with people and give back to the community. When queried as prospective recruits, many law enforcement officers honestly say that their chief reason for becoming a peace officer is the desire to help others.

The "protect" side of law enforcement often requires the servant officer to transform into warrior mode to stay alive. The daily threat of bodily harm requires confidence and courage combined with physical and mental toughness. Every officer must be emotionally prepared to make tough "life-and-death" decisions in a fraction of a second. Making the right choice(s) quickly in a rapidly changing environment increases the chance that the citizen and the warrior safely emerge from the confrontation. Though arrest and detention of the criminal element constitute only a small percentage of the average police officer's day, the significance of the task is off of the chart.

Serve and protect reminds me of a law enforcement version of the yin and the yang, two principles which are opposed to one another and as such are also complimentary. For maximum efficiency, one cannot exist without the other. Enforcement officers that are tough as steel, both physically and mentally, are a necessary component of this business. The challenge of finding human beings who can balance being an "appropriate bad ass," yet not an abuser, can be problematic and quite complicated.

Who You Hire Matters

Think for a minute about the type of people that public safety seeks to employ. Law enforcement seeks those who are self-confident, decisive, passionate, mentally tough, and assertive—goal oriented problem solvers who like to work independently. They are critical thinkers and most are very innovative, but at the same time strong team players. Add to this the attributes of intelligence, courage, honesty, good character, persuasiveness, and strong work ethic, and you have the DNA of many successful law enforcement heroes.

I believe that a peace officer's psychological fit toward the profession that they are joining is considerably more important than their base of knowledge. There is a direct correlation between how someone visualizes the law enforcement profession and how they introspectively view themselves. If personal beliefs, values, attitude, and attributes match those of the chosen profession, the applicant's confidence and performance are categorically reinforced.

In the first year alone, law enforcement spends hundreds of hours and approximately $125,000.00 to recruit, test, investigate, polygraph, interview, hire, train, and equip new officers. Logic dictates that an investment of this magnitude would certainly yield significant success in screening out unpleasant and flawed candidates. For the most part, public safety screening processes are highly effective. The overwhelming majority of those who make it past the eliminators turn out to be exceptional officers with strong skills and high moral values.

However, as we shall see, an unacceptable number of officers manage to evade the rigorous screening process with disastrous results.

Exceptional Training

Once hired, the public safety profession takes these talented individuals and makes them even stronger through basic training and cultural indoctrination. The new recruit is taught community policing, command bearing, voice control, physical restraint techniques, how to deploy weapons, and execute tactics designed to provide the upper hand during any confrontation.

Remarkable preparation and fabulous training teaches officers how to control situations and end up with winning outcomes. The effects of the mental and physical enhancements are mostly positive and create professional workers whose skill set enables them to be typically much stronger performers than the average citizen. Law enforcement continually builds on these strengths through in-service and specialized training. In theory, we take someone who already has many advantages and then make them significantly better.

When applied properly, highly regarded officers will use their heightened skill levels for competitive advantage and victory over adversaries. The drawback is that this incredible training also inadvertently boosts the skill level of the incorrigible within the ranks. In this case, the result is a magnificently trained incorrigible who can use their amplified abilities to cause harm and destruction within.

A Few Are In the Business for the Wrong Reasons

Long-term officers are inspired and encouraged by the excitement of the profession. Saving lives, solving problems, maintaining order, and putting evil people in jail offers private rewards that arouse positive energy. The personal satisfaction that accompanies doing the right thing and making a difference in society helps to propel the respectable officer back to work day after day.

What is it then that allows some of these cutting-edge people to become toxic and troublesome? Unfortunately, there are a small percentage of people who seek law enforcement as a profession for all the wrong reasons. The misguided try to make up for their personal inadequacies by joining a profession that automatically bestows upon them a large dose of status and authority. The symbolism of the uniform, badge, and gun can greatly enhance their undesirable characteristics of power, control, and ego.

Some of these individuals are incompetents who are trying to convince themselves and others that they matter. The inept and ineffectual lack appropriate confidence and need the reassurance that they are indeed somebody important. Whether spoken or internalized, these people far too often demand respect, and feel validated by the badge and its authority. Once promoted, the toxic often feel that their magnificence has been affirmed through the attainment of rank and position.

We will refer to the most egregious of these offenders as "power addicts." Power addicts usually have a deep seated need to dominate everything and dictate to everyone. Some power addicts are easily spotted, but many are able to cleverly hide their dysfunction for months or even years. Once immersed in law enforcement, power addicts tend to become abusive ego maniacs. They are likely to exploit, manipulate, and misapply the enormous influence and authority entrusted to law enforcement. Some power addicts engage in violent criminal activity, but more often those that have slipped through the extensive screening processes exhibit behaviors that range from obnoxious and offensive to cruel and vicious.

Impact of Organizational Culture

Values, background, passion, personal drive, and high skill combine to make the law enforcement culture filled with employees who should be capable of phenomenal accomplishment.

Extraordinary day-to-day experiences offer an opportunity for the average first responder to become an almost superhuman problem solver.

However, all is not peaches and cream in Camelot. The extraordinary demands of the profession can flip-flop between favorable and undesirable. Let's examine five unique and significant cultural influences that challenge law enforcement officers throughout their career:

Societal Expectations - Officers shoulder an astonishing amount of responsibility, anxiety, and stress. The desire to perform admirably makes much of this burden self-imposed, but enforcers face significant psychological challenges from the people they serve. The community expects their heroes to be held to a higher standard. Enforcers live in a fishbowl world where every move and every word is examined, analyzed, and even photographed. Most successful officers manage this difficulty, but the strain of the ever-present burden usually takes some toll, and manifests itself very differently in various people.

Enormous Power and Influence - The average new officer is very young and mostly inexperienced in the ways of the world. Once they complete training, law enforcement newbies are thrust upon society in uniform, with a badge, gun, handcuffs, baton, pepper spray, and a vehicle equipped to make it clear to everyone that they are in charge. The rookie is then sent to do battle with a mantra similar to "do whatever you have to do" to get the job done and come home alive.

Many citizens yield respectfully, and the officer experiences what it is like to take away personal liberty. He or she also experiences what it is like to be in command, and the opposite sex becomes intrigued by the enhanced exhibition of confidence. This newfound clout and influence over fellow human beings can overwhelm the naïve. All officers must learn how to manage the enormous amount of power and control. Some manage the authority satisfactorily, but many experience repercussions both at home and on the job. Humility evades some and their inner destructive behavior takes center stage.

Pressure to Always Win and Never Lose. We all know that no one is perfect. People sometimes make mistakes and bad decisions. Unfortunately for the mere mortal cop, in their work environment, they are expected to always be right. They are taught and need to understand that law and order must win repetitively. Though it is not possible to enjoy victory every single time, there are good reasons why the mindset is in play for law enforcement. Unfortunately, when officers err at an unsuitable time in the wrong situation, people can and often will lose their livelihood, a family member, or their life.

Though no one is flawless, and everyone blunders, the burden of repetitively pursuing near perfection can be exhausting. The effects of the "cannot lose" compulsion are cumulative. Again, every officer processes and copes with this expectation differently. Some find that the continual pressure chips away at an emotional layer of armor that acted as their protective shield. Those that experience the worst of this phenomenon may feel high stress and emotional exhaustion.

Ever-Present Negativity - The job of the officer is filled with conflict and contradiction. Many of the people that officers are sworn to serve and protect actually despise them and may try to inflict damage and/or deadly harm. Even the average everyday resident has ambivalent feelings toward the officer. If the police are helping to solve a serious problem, they may be perceived as a good influence. But, if officers censor behavior, take away personal resources, or remove a citizens' freedom by putting them in jail, they are likely to be viewed negatively. Add to this mix the adversarial nature and lack of support from the legal system, and the result can be a perplexing and toxic stew.

Considerable interaction with the most dreadful elements of society also modifies the essence of the officer. Regular doses of violence involving homicide, suicide, rape, and assault, combined with child abuse, sex crimes, burglary, and general disagreeableness will make some skeptical of the goodness of mankind. Others become so pessimistic that they no longer see a well-adjusted picture of society.

Necessity Teaches Cops to be Skeptical and Look for the Undesirable. The school of hard knocks teaches law officers that things are not always as they appear. Nearly all suspects and many witnesses deliberately lie and mislead investigators. Effective detectives learn to read between the lines, evaluate body language, and find the fault that often lies beneath the surface. Suspicion and cynicism can easily become the daily companion of the officer. In other words, the public safety business can teach officers to find fault with most everything and everybody.

The volume, flagrancy, and vastness of the deceit can cause some officers to lose faith in all things virtuous. The cultural paradigms of "everyone lies" and "everyone always tries to get one over on me" makes it nearly impossible for coworkers to genuinely trust one another. Power addicts and others with psychological deficiencies may use their suspicion and contempt for humanity as perverse justification for abusive exploits within the agency.

Human Fallibility

How easy is it for the law enforcement mindset to jump the track? What happens when the paradox of unintended consequences infects the psyche of those who may be inadequate in the area of sturdy character and strong moral values? If the dark sides of the useful qualities become dominant, then the internal compass guiding their actions can easily switch from beneficial to undesirable.

Let's examine the blurring or even the crossing over of the very thin line that separates constructive desirable attributes and behavior from the wicked and vile:

The Very Thin Line

Desired Aspects	Antonym
Mentally tough & assertive	Domineering over-aggressiveness can nourish the **Bully**
Confident & decisive	Overconfidence and rigidity can easily turn into **Arrogance**
Command presence	Low emotional intelligence plus fear can be the root of **Indecisiveness**
Character and morality	Flaws can lead to corruption or **Moral Bankruptcy**
Team player and goal oriented	"Yes persons" who hide their **Incompetent** performance
Strong work ethic	Too much control and one can become a **Micromanager**
Persuasive communicator	Acerbic slickness can turn into **Untruthfulness** and deception
Unpretentiousness	Humbleness and humility may be masking a **Suck-up**

Close

Those who thrive and survive the complexity of the law enforcement experience do in fact become much like the hero's described earlier in this chapter. However, as we have discovered, there is indeed a fine line in law enforcement between being a hero and being a power addict. Undesirable traits and behaviors are easily masked by the evil, and often end up surfacing as toxic and debilitating conduct.

Many of those that create an atmosphere of negativity and dissention leave the policing business for ventures that are more suitable to their desires and abilities. However, far too often the power addicts achieve their personal agenda and everyone in their path; individuals, their organizations, and the community ends up paying dearly. Public safety agencies of the future will be well-served if they learn to improve their ability to discern the true aptitudes of the people that they employ.

Chapter 3

WHY DOES TOXICITY SEEM TO BE A PROMOTIONAL ADVANTAGE

In the ideal world, all law enforcement promotions would be based solely on merit and the potential for supervisory competence. After all, promotions are most often viewed as rewards for past performance, are they not? If we asked a room full of managers why they believed they had been promoted what would they say? I strongly suspect that nearly everyone would respond; they earned it. Thank goodness that talented, dedicated people who perform ethically often times are promoted.

The problem is that we do not live in an ideal world and life is not always fair. Many people who do great work are passed over on a consistent basis. Circumstances other than accomplishments play a vital role in choosing who is selected for a particular job.

The majority of law enforcement supervisors and managers are truly outstanding. However, straight talk dictates that we have to admit that nearly every organization has some really bad actors in leadership positions. Why do law enforcement employees with toxic tendencies achieve positions of significance in the public safety workplace? This chapter will focus on the relationship between office politics, cultural idiosyncrasies, and the rise of the toxic abuser.

Political CYA

"Covering your backside" plays a large role in the life of nearly every toxic performer. As we discussed earlier, the toxic do not play fair. Their mindset revolves around manipulating every situation to their advantage—what's mine is mine and what's yours is mine. Political "grab ass" is part of their modus operandi. Doing favors "For our mutual benefit" and "You scratch my back I'll scratch yours" can become standard operating procedure.

The higher one travels up the organizational ladder, the more political factors impact choices and calculations. At the top level of the food chain, Chiefs or Sheriffs must exercise mastery over politics in order to retain their employment. Think of it this way; the primary function of every Sheriff is to do whatever it takes to get re-elected. If the Sheriff loses re-election, they no longer have a job. A Police Chief is also most often accountable to elected officials. If the Chief alienates the City Council, Mayor, or local Board, he or she will likely be dismissed.

The spine of the executive determines just how much they are willing to compromise. A few will stand strong and do the right thing regardless of the consequences. To boost their ego and buttress their empire, many will fall victim to the enticement of propagating the false idea that no issues or troubles exist under their watch. All of the way up the chain of command, there is pressure to spin things so that it appears as though everything is going great. To the toxic, sugarcoating or concealing issues will ensure that all is well "on paper" and everything is running smoothly under their command.

When pleasing the politicians becomes the top focus in the workplace, ethical corruption takes over as standard operating procedure. If power or influence is distributed solely as a reward for being on the executive's team, cultural integrity is compromised for all the wrong reasons. When politics reign supreme, promotions and perks become an ugly byproduct, awarded to those who appear to be the most closely aligned with the toxic boss.

Hyper Ego

Is there an ego problem in public safety? Straight talk demands that we answer in the affirmative. As we discussed in Chapter 1, there are cultural phenomena that induce law enforcement to pursue the delusion of creating employees who are as close to perfect as possible. Unfortunately, some officers lose their ego equilibrium (those in the sports arena would say that they believe their own press clippings) and end up with hyper egos that really do need to be checked.

Serving officers will likely recognize co-workers with the hyper ego I am talking about; they have seen them in action. The hyper-ego officer, whose cocky attitude and nasty demeanor causes them to fight more than they talk. This guy or gal alienates fellow workers, and usually leads the shift in citizen complaints. Professional officers feel uncomfortable when they witness the hyper-ego humiliate the public or use excessive force because they felt the need to unnecessarily exercise their authority. Hyper-ego cops place professional officers in the uncomfortable predicament of ignoring the wrong, intervening, or reporting the misconduct and being labeled a snitch.

One of the major problems facing the law enforcement business today is that far too often the overly cocky rise up the promotional ladder. When officers are influence hungry, then they continuously seek more and more power. As they rise through the ranks, their hyper ego swells, their destructive influence magnifies, and they turn their vitriol to those who make them feel vulnerable inside their own agency.

Toxic hyper-ego managers are motivated by self-interest. They need and seek personal reinforcement that everything is "the best it's ever been" under their stewardship. The hyper-ego manager creates and thrives in a "love fest" environment. "Yes sir, yes sir, anything you say, sir," is the steady diet that they feed their superiors, as well as what they expect from subordinates. In their own mind, these losers with authority justify their arrogance and actions by internalizing some version of "I must be pretty damn good—after all I am the shift commander, Captain, Deputy Chief, or Chief."

The hyper ego is frequently public with their disdain of co-workers whom they view as insignificant **or** as a threat. They will use any tactic and play dirty pool to maintain their position or increase their ascension. Hyper ego toxic bosses dismiss poor morale and blame all problems on a few disgruntled malcontents and incompetents. Hyper ego managers in high positions are likely to dismiss tools and methods such as 360 evaluations, or any kind of feedback that exposes flaws and highlights their personal deficiencies.

Junkyard Dog Theory

Nearly all law enforcement promotions come from within the existing organization. Although the Chief or Sheriff is sometimes brought in from an outside agency, most high ranking supervisors have started at the bottom of their organizations and worked their way up. Competition is fierce, as there are normally a large number of candidates vying for only a very few slots. Ambition and long odds sometimes make promotional opportunities an intense competition between the best of the best.

Regrettably, toxic competitors often use underhanded tactics to gain an advantage. Since toxic behaviors such as destroying the competition, often do help obtain promotions, in some agencies they become the key to prosperity and winning the prize. Toxic people who have been through the promotion wars repetitively become as tough as junkyard dogs. These dogs usually become more vicious and despicable over time as they gain proficiency.

Since more is at stake at every level, the junkyard dog phenomenon becomes more intense and extreme as competitors rise closer to the top of the organization. The end result is that many organizations have a whole group of junkyard dogs at the top of the pile. The junkyard dog that ends up with the biggest bone is likely to have proven to be the "meanest of the mean," rather than the "best of the best."

Tricks That Toxic Co-Workers Use To Get Ahead

What promotion factors determine who gets advanced in your organization? We all know that there are many constructive and appropriate pursuits that can help with career progression. Readers of this book should understand that toxic competitors are not using the same rulebook as everyone else. A problem arises when the dirty tricks of the poisonous antagonists lead them to success. Let's examine a number of techniques that influence promotional achievement. The weight that each of the listed attributes carry is dependent upon the level of toxicity of those who are in charge.

The Very Thin Line

Positive and Helpful Activity	Toxic Tricks
Do your job well	Take credit for other people's ideas
Improve education	Always say "Yes," or "What ever you say, you are the best"
Be a team player	Slice and dice the competition— make opponents look bad
Obtain a mentor	Ask self-serving questions to build the ego of the boss
Acquire new knowledge and skills	Quantify results in great detail to fool upper management
Work well with people	Focus on not making enemies of those those in high places
Maintain a positive outlook	Pretend to have a positive out look while being secretly destructive
Volunteer	Work extra hard at establishing a close close personal bond with the boss
Be a problem solver	Never question anything
Build your network	Disingenuous socialization with superiors
Get noticed	Practice self-promotion. Frequently talk about what a great job "I" do
Ask for more responsibility	Demonstrates willingness to punish and do the dirty work
Make constructive suggestions	Spreads rumors and lies about challengers

The Buck Starts or Stops Here

It is quite clear that the law enforcement executive, responsible for every aspect and function under their command, sets the tone, implements the vision, and provides direction for the agency. In large measure, the agency will reflect the attitude and demeanor of the person at the top of the organizational chart. A strong appropriate leader with excellent skills will most often correlate with effective organizational performance. The opposite is equally true.

The CEO, Chief, or Sheriff determines whether or not they have toxic offenders within their own house. Failure to control or eliminate toxic behavior essentially excuses and emboldens the practitioner. For all intents and purposes, some in leadership positions encourage, or at least tolerate, the unscrupulous conduct. Tolerating the inappropriate behavior amounts to a blessing that promotes its existence and allows it to flourish. In fact, any boss that knowingly accepts, fosters, or condones toxic behavior should be held fully accountable for the mayhem that they are facilitating.

Close

The enormous amount of power and influence that law officers have at their disposal puts them at high risk of becoming an egotistical zealot. Emotional deficiencies make it impossible for some to hold steady when confronted with the hazards of intoxicating influence. Sadly, if your agency has toxic managers at or near the top of the organization, and you probably do, the cultural anomalies and despicable methods described in this Chapter likely have been re-enforced and institutionalized.

Chapter 4

STANDARD OPERATION PROCEDURES

&

TACTICS FOR TOXIC MANAGEMENT

Understand that toxic bosses are using unseemly and often discriminatory management to control the perceived minions within the ranks. In the real world toxic bosses can intimidate employees by inappropriately using their dominant position. Often times the toxic boss is authorized to hire, promote, transfer, or fire their subordinates. Employees are often rightfully fearful for their careers and for their jobs.

The goal of the toxic manager is to maintain superiority and protect their position. They regulate and manipulate their work environment by driving unwanted individuals and dissent underground. If the perceived menace can be beaten into submission, the toxic manager can more easily fool others into believing that the disagreement either never existed, or that the hazard went away harmlessly.

Force, threat, and intimidation are the gold standards of toxic management. In a private setting, the toxic frequently take advantage of the differential of positional power to inflict damage behind closed doors under the guise of management confidentiality. One-on-one backstabbing makes it easy to ensure that no fact checking occurs, since no one is present to dispute the vocalized rubbish.

The public destruction of reputation can be just as devastating and acute. What follows is a discussion of some of the more open and common suppression and control techniques frequently employed by the toxic manager.

Whack-A-Mole

How many of our readers remember the children's game whack-a-mole? The person with dominion and control over the game has a mallet that allows him or her to pound the plastic moles as they randomly appear. The timing and potency of the blow induces the mole to retreat as other moles then popup. The departure of each threat allows the gamer to reestablish tranquility and superiority.

In the toxic law enforcement environment, the manager uses a workplace version of whack-a-mole to control direct reports. By virtue of positional authority and influence, whack-a-mole managers have many formidable career destruction devices at their disposal. Toxic whack-a-mole bosses often believe that it is their right and their duty to knock some sense into the perceived delinquents. Most will not hesitate to bring out a big stick to restore order if they perceive the tug of lurking chaos.

Public servant whack-a-mole is very common. The game in law enforcement works like this; when officers gain a bit of confidence and stick their heads up to take a chance, the manager thumps them hard in an attempt to bash 'em silly. The golden rule of toxic whack-a-mole is that one good abusive smack SHOULD teach a reasonably smart wrongdoer not to repeat the unwelcome behavior. For the hardheaded or slow learner, the whacks tend to become more frequent, much more forceful, and more public.

The venomous believe that frequently and vigorously attacking the problem person will eventually cause even the unwise to retreat. Most reasonably intelligent people will utilize the natural instincts of future pain avoidance and embarrassment. Regrettably, the thrashing of a beat down is effective whether administered in a private or a public setting. Whack-a-mole management takes advantage of the fact that most people seek to avoid personal attacks, evade conflict, and are uncomfortable with the implication that they may not be viewed as positive and productive employees.

Disgruntled Employees

What happens when toxic bosses face disagreement or a dilemma that has the potential to tilt their halo or dim the glorious glow they want their superiors to appreciate? As discussed previously, in the minds of the toxic, the problem is most certainly not due to any fault of their own. One of the most common methods used by the unscrupulous manager to alleviate a situation like this will be to place the blame squarely upon the shoulders of a scapegoat or patsy.

Prevailing toxic theory is that a few disgruntled bad apples are the cause of law enforcement turmoil within an agency. Blaming and demonizing a few troublemakers is an attempt to make it clear to all that culpability lays within the problematic individuals. The disgruntled whiner scheme is often a ruse deceitfully used to confuse the issue. Denouncing frustrated employees makes it easy for the toxic bosses to frame and regulate the opinion of the misinformed.

Reputable employees who are properly disciplined and treated with respect may grouse a bit, but most will understand that their performance could have been better, get over it, and rejoin the team. In truth, malcontented employees are dissatisfied for a reason. Some workers do complain incessantly because of their internal disposition, but it is far more likely that the organization's unhappy employees have rightful grounds to be upset.

Death by Documentation

Respectable and experienced managers all know that "document, document, document" is one of the core doctrines of effective management. Appropriate documentation of professional success boosts employee confidence while giving credit where credit is due. Positive recognition is undoubtedly tied to workplace success.

Maintaining a notation of unfavorable performance can be equally important. Written reinforcement is helpful in the development of performance improvement plans, counseling, and corrective actions. Progressive disciplinary proceedings often rely on previous records when there is a need to initiate termination proceedings.

Troubles arise when toxic bosses wrongly use a legitimate management tool to facilitate their grimy work. An unscrupulous manager building a case for termination poses a dangerous minefield for employees. Outright fabrication of fact is more common that many can imagine. The misrepresentation is then transferred to paper and presented to the accused for "verification" by way of the obligatory signature. Unless there is a witness, recording, or other evidence, it is extraordinarily difficult for a victim of this type of abuse to dispute the supervisor's manipulation of the event.

It is also quite easy for the spiteful manager to slip a nasty note, email, or false document of accusation into the file of an unsuspecting target. The memo will follow the unwary prey throughout the years. The content and vileness of the letter can undeniably be fatal to career advancement. Underhanded use of no rehire recommendations and unacceptable references can contribute to financial instability over the lifetime of the victim.

Selective Memory

Each of us is engaged in a daily balancing act of what to forget and what to remember. Stress, information overload, competing priorities, and life events all impact our ability to recall data. Medical issues can cause retention deterioration, and it is well known that many older adults show age-related reductions in memory.

Sometimes two people fail to communicate properly. It seems human nature that we have a tendency to remember events in a way that are favorable to us and our actions. In other words, it is very easy to receive and process only what we want to hear. Toxic managers, on the other hand, have a nasty habit of frequently remembering some facts while apparently forgetting those that are troublesome.

The dishonest manager uses selective memory conveniently, particularly in instances where they were incorrect. Excuses such as "you misunderstood" or "you remembered that wrong" are some of the least invasive of these cons. You "never gave that to me" or "I was not notified" can be the next steps up the devious ladder of mistruth. The most despicable examples of malicious selective memory may be the infamous renunciations of, "I never said that" or "that never happened."

Convenient memory loss is simply a form of manipulative untruthfulness. It is an assault on interpersonal decency that simultaneously violates the implications of the employer-employee contract. If no email, witness, or formal document exists, the victim has virtually no way to refute the detrimental, fictitious assertions.

You're Not on My Team

It seems likely that most of us will generally agree that the majority of law enforcement employees are good people with wholesome motives and habits. Noble causes, integrity, collaboration, and doing the right thing are professional cornerstones that draw many into the profession of public safety. The experience of belonging to the brotherhood or sisterhood usually lasts a lifetime, and almost never leaves the innermost essence of most law enforcement officers.

But, just as predictable as the sun rising in the morning, the toxic uses this powerful part of officer psyche to control, divide, and conquer. The dreaded label of troublemaker, or failing to support what the organization stands for, will simultaneously attack individual confidence, isolate the targeted officer, and marginalize the effectiveness of the professed enemy. Undeniably, being deemed "not a team player" can become the career kiss of death.

Toxic administrators will often affix the label of disloyalty upon their target as they attempt to paint the picture of the offending individual as "you're not on my team." The self-perceived King demands and expects absolute loyalty to the ruler. The inherent fallacy of this thinking escapes those who tend to see themselves as the almighty. I will offer that no one has the right to twist the concept of loyalty into some perverted unquestioned allegiance to an individual. It is possible to disagree with the organization's leaders, yet still be steadfast to the mission. Loyalty and fidelity in law enforcement should be the province of self, community, and agency first.

Blame Everything on the Higher Ups

It is often said that the hierarchal structure of law enforcement mirrors that of the military. Nearly all law enforcement agencies utilize a rigid, paramilitary chain of command system to manage day-to-day processes. Addressing an issue outside the chain of command is rare and is almost never considered acceptable behavior. Directives often come from the top down, and every leader understands that duty will sometimes obligate them to support and implement unpopular policies.

Toxic managers like to use the chain of command as handy justification for their misdeeds. Misfit bosses takes advantage of the fact that they can stifle questions or dissent by misusing positional clout. Toxic bosses make it clear that questioning of their authority will be accompanied by severe consequences. Employees get the message that anyone who dares to cross the boss by taking concerns to the next level does so at their own peril.

A second version of this same tactic involves blaming every uncomfortable decision or action on the higher ups. Toxic bosses insist on quelling the disturbance at their level. They will also issue improper decrees in the name of someone close to the top echelon. After all, who would be foolish enough to question a high-ranking official when he or she was the originator of the order or concept? Sounds a lot like political suicide, does it not? The blame game provides a comfortable level of insulation to the toxic boss's wrongdoings.

Close

Many career progressions have been halted by standing up to the boss. Ill-mannered and vulgar management practices chip away at the core issues of trust, teamwork, and collegiality. It takes extraordinary courage, determination, and energy to continue to wage battle against the demoralization that accompanies the standard operating procedures and tactics used by toxic managers. Civil liability, legal debates, moral predicaments, ethical dilemmas, health issues, and lost career opportunities are among the many potential consequences that can surface when an officer must continuously run uphill doing battle with these noxious demons.

15 Ways to Know A Toxic Bully When You See One

Demonstrates poor impulse control - short fuse

Curses, yells, or uses loud-in-your-face aggressive language

Attempts to intimidate others with their size or physical aggressiveness

Purposely instills fear in co-workers in order to gain an advantage

Shows intense and immediate anger in insignificant situations

Threatens that they possess the power to halt career progression

Delights in humiliating, demoralizing or embarrassing subordinates in a public format

*Maliciously targets those they perceive as either weak **or** as a threat*

Threatens bodily harm

Speaks softly and tries to project a calm image until they explode

Harshly critiques ideas and suggestions of co-workers or subordinates

Acts intolerant

Shuts down conversation and discussion

Projects their own poor self-image and negative thoughts onto others

Sabotages peers who are competitors for advancement

Sends a message to others by making a public example of a victim

Covers up their own blowups

Chapter 5

TOXICITY OF THE CAUSTIC BULLY

General Dwight D. Eisenhower once said, "You do not lead by hitting people over the head – that's assault, not leadership." The intensity of the terror from a caustic bully causes work trauma that poisons and destroys the culture of an organization. Excessively antagonistic and corrosive language from those in powerful positions devastates productivity and damages emotional and physical health.

Bullying inflicts emotional violence upon a victim. Though co-workers may not be able to see physical scarring, the damage can be devastating. Harsh, threatening, and caustic communications from so-called leaders cultivate employees who are withdrawn, walk on eggshells, and who dread coming to work. If employees are hesitant to offer ideas, speak freely, and generally engage only in safe non-controversial activity, then it is a sure bet that bullies are trekking the halls with impunity.

Unfortunately, management bullies are an all-too-common problem in the law enforcement environment. Workplace bullying affects 35% of employees, according to a 2010 survey by the Workplace Bullying Institute (WBI), a Washington State nonprofit organization. In fact, several of the bullying victims in an agency may actually be some of the brightest employees on the payroll. Toxic bosses in powerful positions who feel deficient or vulnerable may select their targets for unfair treatment due to the victim's advanced abilities and competence. Perceived threats to career progression may cause the bully to target individuals simply because they believe that a more skilled co-worker will interfere with their own career ambitions.

The stories that follow are just a few examples of inappropriate conduct by toxic bully bosses that far too many of us have witnessed throughout our careers.

Evacuate as Directed that's an Order

A police agency is experiencing a shots fired / hostage situation in a crowded apartment complex. Numerous supervisors from different disciplines are being called to the scene to assist with the situation. A Watch Commander has control of the overall incident. The SWAT team commander and the Watch Commander are in the command post making decisions and navigating the situation as circumstances dictate.

A Uniform Operations Lieutenant enters the command post to brief the Watch Commander regarding the current situation. The Lieutenant and the Watch Commander discuss securing the safety of citizens who live in the apartment complex. The Watch Commander indicates that he believes that evacuating citizens from adjacent apartments would be a wise and prudent course of action. The Lieutenant suggests that it may be best for the Police to have citizen's hunkers down in place rather than risking their removal.

The healthy and appropriate conversation between two of the on-scene supervisors continued with the Lieutenant professionally reiterating his belief that it would be better to leave those potentially in the line of fire to *shelter in place*. Suddenly, the SWAT team commander, who was not directly involved in the discussion regarding perimeter security, rises to his feet, invades the Lieutenant's personal space, and blows up by angrily and aggressively yelling "EVACUATE AS DIRECTED LIEUTENANT, and THAT IS AN ORDER!" The Lieutenant, obviously offended and visibly upset, responds, "Yes sir," and quickly leaves the command post. The relationship between the SWAT Commander and the Lieutenant was permanently damaged.

If faced with the scenario described above, what would you have done?

- *Was the shift Lieutenant out of line when he offered an alternative to the Watch Commander's verbal directive?*

- *Was the SWAT team commander on target when he quelled what he perceived as insubordination?*

- *If you were the Watch Commander described above, what conversation, if any, would you have with the shift Lieutenant following the confrontation?*

- *If you were the Watch Commander described above, what conversation, if any, would you have had with the SWAT commander after this confrontation?*

Throw the Recording Device Against the Wall

A new Special Agent for a U.S. Federal law enforcement position completed his initial six months of training and was placed on one-year probationary period. The new agent was never assigned to a Senior Agent for training and was given only minimum guidance, which consisted mostly of how to fill out forms and how to keep his mouth shut.

The Special Agent in Charge (SAIC) assigned a different Agent who had just gotten out of basic training, as the squad supervisor. It didn't take long for the young and inexperienced supervisor to start finding fault with the performance of his new subordinates. While working on a case with another Federal agency, some confusion arose over investigative practices. The subject of the investigation called the SAIC and made a complaint against the probationary agent. The new supervisor was made aware of the complaint and told to investigate the behavior.

A meeting was held between the probationary agent, the new supervisor and the Assistant Special Agent in Charge (ASAIC). The interview lasted all of two minutes and resulted in nothing. Months later, a second incident involving questionable investigative technique came to light that involved an Assistant U.S. Attorney. The new supervisor called the probationary agent and told him to report to the office immediately. Due to the nature of their thorny relationship, the probationary officer felt the need to take a tape recorder into the meeting with the supervisor.

When he entered the new supervisor's office, the probationary agent was ordered to "sit" in front of the supervisor. Another agent from the office was present for the meeting. The new supervisor noticed the recording device right away. The new supervisor told the probationary agent to turn the recorder off and put it away. When the probationary officer refused to put the recording device away, the new supervisor began loudly shouting for the probationer to turn it off. Again, the probationer refused.

The new supervisor got up, jerked the recording device from the probationer's hand and threw it across the room where it smashed into many pieces. The stunned probationary agent then requested that the SAIC be brought into the room for the remainder of the meeting. The probationary agent turned away from the new supervisor and attempted to leave to get the SAIC. The probationary agent felt a hand grab his shoulder, and he was quickly spun around. The new supervisor seized the agent with both hands by the front of his shirt, lifted the probationary agent off of the floor and slammed him against the office wall.

This of course caused quite a racket and people started coming toward the office. The new supervisor released the probationary agent and left the room quickly. The probationary agent, startled and confused, did not know what to do. Eventually, the probationary agent went to the ASAIC and told him what had occurred. Both agents went to the office of the SAIC.

The SAIC took no action at all. When asked why no action would be taken, the SAIC initially refused to say why. The probationary agent told the SAIC that he felt like the new supervisor owed him an apology. The SAIC flatly refused the request. The SAIC told the probationary officer in no uncertain terms that he, the SAIC, was supporting the supervisor because he was the supervisor.

- *Was it acceptable for the new agent to bring a tape recorder into the meeting with his supervisor?*

- *Should the new agent have turned off the recording device when he was directed to do so by the supervisor?*

- *What course of action should the new agent pursue following the assault and battery?*

- *If you were the new agent, what would you do after the SAIC told you that it would not be in your best interest to pursue the matter up the chain of command?*

You're Insubordinate!

A Sergeant observes a traffic violation that nearly results in an automobile crash. The Sergeant conducts a traffic stop with the offending vehicle. The driver of the offending vehicle is an average citizen who is visibly shaken. The driver apologizes and indicates that he made an innocent mistake. The driver reveals that though he looked in both directions, he just did not see the oncoming vehicle.

During the aforementioned traffic stop, a second vehicle screeched to a stop behind the Sergeant. A female exited the vehicle and began to aggressively approach the scene. The Sergeant asked the female how he could assist her. The female is very irritated and begins shouting "What is he going to be charged with" and "I WILL be in court." The Sergeant explains to the citizen that thankfully no one was hurt during the near crash, and that there would be no formal charges. The female erupted in anger screaming "That's not fair" and "If it were me I would be put under the jail." The Sergeant attempted to calm the woman, provided his name and shield number, and left the scene.

Approximately forty-five minutes later, the shift Lieutenant called the Sergeant and requested a meeting in the Lieutenant's office. Upon the Sergeant's arrival, the Lieutenant indicated that he had taken a telephone call from a witness who was unhappy with the way the stop was conducted. The Sergeant was asked to explain the circumstances of the traffic stop.

After the Sergeant provided details of the stop, the Lieutenant made the statement, "I want you to go to the judicial official's office and obtain a summons for that guy." The Sergeant politely told the Lieutenant that he had no plans to bring charges against the driver. The Sergeant further explained that due to the circumstances, he felt that no traffic charges were warranted.

The Lieutenant, perceiving disobedience, becomes angry and sternly said, "You don't understand, that is an order!" The Sergeant explained to the Lieutenant that he was exercising discretion, that he was confident that his on-scene decision was right, and that he would not initiate charges just to placate someone who wished to make a citizen complaint.

The Lieutenant's face got red, he burst out of his chair, aggressively approached the Sergeant and while putting a finger directly in the Sergeant's face shouts, "You're insubordinate!" The Sergeant calmly replies "You're incompetent, and out of line."

The Lieutenant became so spastic that he began to pace around the room yelling, "You're insubordinate; that is an order, you son-of-a-#@!!%, I am charging you with insubordination!" The Lieutenant, who by this time had completely lost control of himself, continued to curse and yell "Damn you, son-of-a- #@!!%, I'm charging you with insubordination." "I told you to bring charges against that man."

- *If you were the Sergeant described above, would you have brought charges against the "failure to yield" driver when directed to do so by your Lieutenant?*

- *How would you react once the Lieutenant became angry, put his finger in your face, and called you insubordinate?*

- *How would you react when the Lieutenant totally lost his cool, cursing, threatening, and stomping around the room?*

How Does the Toxic Bully Affect the Workplace?

Dictionary.com . . . defines a bully as a blustering, quarrelsome, overbearing person who habitually badgers and intimidates.

Let's take a closer look at some of the most critical ways that a toxic bully manager negatively impacts the law enforcement workplace.

Promotes an unsafe work environment: The caustic bully can cause treacherous conditions in their work sector. Yelling, screaming, and out of control behavior is used to intimidate and influence the actions of co-workers. Sudden, aggressive outbursts by the bully put everyone in their path on edge. The behavior generates anxiety and stress; workers will be treading lightly trying not to trigger an outburst. Many times, peers or direct reports will duck, hide, or avoid the bully for fear that they will set the offender off and experience the full brunt of the beast.

Caustic managers create employee animosity. Mistreatment produces anger and resentment. An angry workforce increases conflict, mistrust, and hostility. Threatening behavior may lead to emotional injury, physical injury, or tragically even suicide and homicide. The more egregious scenarios end with the caustic bully physically assaulting the work victim. The severity of the battery can trigger death, arrest, criminal proceedings, and civil liability for both the worker and the employer.

Sends morale down the tubes: Victims of the caustic bully manager will be very unhappy and likely bitter. The behavior of the bully commonly erodes confidence. Sufferers may experience low self-esteem, feel paralyzed, powerless, and helpless. Productivity is diminished, as time is wasted by employees thinking about the situation, avoiding interaction with others, or seeking support from peers. Teamwork, creativity, synergy, and collaboration are weakened.

Models bad behavior: Employees are learning about and adapting to organizational norms from the moment they arrive on the job. Getting along with others and fitting into the workplace culture are significant components of career success. Being ostracized from the group attacks the fundamental needs of belonging and self-esteem. Many people will do almost anything to protect and sustain the sense of inclusion.

The toxic bully's behavior runs the risk of establishing a workplace model of nastiness. If the masses perceive that the bullying facilitates success, then it is highly likely that at least some will emulate the activity. The outlandish pattern of force, threat, and intimidation sets a very bad example for others to follow. Negative behavior modeled for employees increases the chance that employees will behave badly toward citizens.

Lingering damage: Employees who are bullied may lose faith in their agency. Quite naturally, some will wonder why management allows ill-treatment of what most profess to be their most valuable resource. Employee turnover is likely to increase. It is well known in management circles that disagreement with a bad boss is one of the top reasons workers change jobs. In the case of a caustic bully, unhappy employees often try to flee the misery of their situation. Many will leave the organization altogether, while others will attempt to gain transfers anywhere away from the one with power who is abusing them.

Studies show that the bad deeds of a caustic bully are likely to intensify lost time from work. Victims may use absenteeism as a method of seeking relief. Stress, anxiety, sleep disturbance, and depression can all amplify employee medical problems as workers suffer.

15 Ways to Know A Toxic Arrogant Boss When You See One

Always right, never wrong

Quick indignant temper if challenged

Lack of concern for subordinates

Self-serving attitude and behaviors

Autocratic – knows the answer to everything

Exaggerates self-worth

Insists on blind loyalty

Hypersensitive to suggestion

Talks down to employees with condescending and sarcastic remarks

Projects image that they are in control

Rolls eyes or makes faces when they disagree with what is being said

Mocks and belittles others when they speak

Does not understand nor care about the impact of their behavior toward others

Tend to focus negatively on the person rather than the behavior

Ignores input

Chapter 6

TOXICITY of ARROGANCE

17th century French noble and writer Francois de La Roche-foucauld famously said, "The true meaning of being misled is to believe one finer than the others." Toxic arrogant managers often view themselves at the top of the organizational chart. It is not uncommon for the arrogant to believe that their personal superiority makes them indestructible and untouchable.

Abrasive managers create an indignant workforce filled with discord and suspicion. Animosity and resentment of management creates hostile employees with little incentive to perform at maximum capacity. Hostility increases the likelihood that inappropriate activities will permeate the workplace.

Heavy doses of misguided vanity, pride, and nastiness will produce workers who are withdrawn and less likely to look out for the best interest of the organization. Applying the "crap rolls downhill" theory means that extreme negativity and lack of respect from employer to employee sets a tone of impropriety that the workers may then transfer onto the unsuspecting public.

In the work world of the arrogant, management insists on blind loyalty, with no disagreement, limited input, and muffled conversations. When taken to the extreme, senior executives only promote those who parrot what they say and disenfranchise those who disagree. Most of us have worked for a "pompous ass" boss at one time or another. The following pages may help targets of the arrogant manager understand the egotistical and conceited boss.

The stories that follow are just a few examples of inappropriate conduct by toxic arrogant bosses that far too many of us have witnessed throughout our careers.

Don't You Realize Other People Have Lives?

A high-ranking commander works a schedule that includes nighttime and weekend rotations. The commander reports directly to the Deputy Chief of Police. If an officer in this particular commander's position elects to take a day off, another commander is required to fill in and work the night shift.

Leave and vacation time is granted on a first-come-first-serve basis in this agency. Leave is almost never denied, and there is no minimum time notification standard in place. There is an established on-call schedule (once every ten-weeks) for other commanders so that on-call responsibilities for the week are clearly understood.

On Tuesday morning, the commander notifies the Deputy Chief that he plans to be off on Saturday night. This is done through normal email, voicemail, and paperwork channels. On Tuesday evening when the commander comes to work, he is met in his office by the Deputy Chief and the Chief of Police. The Deputy Chief is visibly upset; face flushed, and his hands are shaking. In a raised trembling voice, the Deputy Chief begins to berate the commander for taking the day off. The Deputy Chief said, "You are so inconsiderate it is unbelievable" and "What do you mean by taking Saturday night off at such a late date?" The Deputy Chief rambles on with further degradation; making such comments as, "You have given insufficient notice" then screaming "DON'T YOU REALIZE PEOPLE HAVE LIVES!"

The stunned commander replies, "I do realize that people have lives, that's why I have requested the day off." The Deputy Chief continues his raging vilification and persists with the verbal maltreatment. At the conclusion of the rant, the commander asks the Deputy Chief, "Are you going to approve the leave request or not?" The Deputy Chief and Chief turn around and leave the office without further comment.

** Guess who was on-call and therefore scheduled to cover the shift on that Saturday night?

- *If you were the commander in the above example, would you have immediately withdrawn your leave request when confronted by the Chiefs?*

- *What would have been your response when the Deputy Chief asked "Don't you realize that people have lives?"*

- *Would you have apologized to the Deputy Chief for the alleged arrogance and inconsiderate behavior?*

- *What conversation, if any, would you have had with the Deputy Chief or Chief after this confrontation?*

Any More Questions?

Public safety officers from this government agency have been chronically underpaid for years. A new Chief takes the helm and declares that he will make every effort to correct the pay issues within the department. A high-ranking commander is assigned to be the architect of a new pay plan. After the plan is conceived, the Chief of Police is made aware that inequities within the plan will make some of his Sergeant's very unhappy. The Chief decides that he needs to address his Sergeants to answer their questions.

Approximately forty (40) Sergeants attend the meeting that the Chief has designated as their time to ask questions. The Chief explains the plan and tells all what a good plan he believes that it is. One long-term Sergeant raises his hand. When called upon, the Sergeant politely states that the plan calls for veteran Sergeants to receive nothing, while young inexperienced Sergeants receive as much as a $10,000 boost in pay. The veteran Sergeant then politely asks the Chief, "When will faithful, long-term employees be rewarded?"

The Chief obviously bristled at the question. The Chief began to aggressively and derogatorily tell the Sergeant that YOU (Sergeant) do not understand how hard I (Chief) have worked on this plan. Over the course of the next two minutes, the Chief of Police publicly and viciously berated the Sergeant. Amongst other disparaging remarks, the Chief insulted the Sergeant's intelligence by saying, "I can't see why YOU don't understand the benefits of the plan," and sarcastically repeats his focus on how hard he (the Chief) had worked to find a solution to the problem.

The auditorium drew deathly quiet. The Sergeant who asked the question and everyone else in the room were shocked and embarrassed. At the conclusion of his diatribe, the Chief asked mockingly, "Anyone ELSE have any questions?" Of course no other questions were asked during this session. The Chief declared that the meeting was over, and stormed out of the room.

- *As a Sergeant in this forum, would you have asked the Chief the question regarding "faithful and long-term" employees? Why, or why not?*

- *If you had asked the question, how would you have responded to the Chief when he deliberately embarrassed and humiliated you in front of your peers?*

- *What conversation, if any, would you have had with your chain of command (including the Chief of Police) following the meeting confrontation?*

- *What effect will this event have upon the 40 Sergeants who work for this Chief?*

*The Answer or the A**hole*

A police department decides that it will embark upon a new crime fighting strategy. As part of the implementation of the philosophy, the Chief of Police makes several transfers and promotions. The new philosophical direction is part and parcel to a crime fighting technique that is based on the analysis of statistics and accountability of supervisors. Two newly promoted Captains are told that it is their responsibility to use all available resources to reduce crime in their assigned areas.

One new Captain is very autocratic and contemptuous. Instead of utilizing teamwork and corroboration, this new Captain sends orders via nasty email and voicemail. He makes it clear that he will hold those under him "accountable" for any transgression or dalliance. In staff meetings with superiors, the new Captain is very vocal with his ideas and suggestions. Almost all of the Captain's sentences begin with "I did," "I have done," or "I have directed my officers" to perform whatever task the Captain sees as pleasing to his superiors.

The department's top brass are impressed by the new Captain's initiative, bravado, and command. It is clear that the administration views the new Captain as "the answer" to all of their concerns. Administration is pleased that the new Captain is exactly what they have been looking for to implement their fresh strategy and make it a success. They praise and elevate the Captain as an example for others to emulate.

Employees who work with or for the new Captain view him as an unreasonable egomaniac with a large dose of a**hole mixed in for good measure.

- *What impact does the aggressive unpleasantness of the Captain have upon the officer's in his area of responsibility?*

- *If you reported to this Captain, how would you respond to his nasty emails and voicemails?*

- *How does the new Captain's threats and strict accountability impact officer productivity in his District?*

- *As a supervisor in this Captain's precinct, what conversation, if any, would you have with the Commander?*

How Does the Toxic Arrogant Boss Affect the Workplace?

Dictionary.com . . . defines arrogance as *making claims or pretensions to superior importance or rights; overbearingly assuming; insolently proud; presumptuous, haughty, imperious, brazen.*

Let's take a closer look at some of the more serious ways that a toxic arrogant manager negatively impacts the law enforcement workplace.

Promotes a hostile workplace culture: The toxic arrogant manager is very concerned about maintaining positional power and authority. In the mind of the toxic, formal authority is not to be breached. Most toxic arrogant managers will establish and fortify a rigid hierarchy that supports their belief that the boss enjoys personal superiority. Continuously highlighting the inequality of an unbalanced workplace structure constructs a tone of antagonism between coworkers.

The toxic arrogant enjoy boosting their ego by displaying and using symbols of power. Plush surroundings, parking spaces, grandiose awards, and bold office decorations are just a few of the physical representations that are used to display preeminence. Empire building is common amongst the arrogant since they often feel that "he who has the most toys has the most influence." The mentality that "mine is bigger and better than yours" creates distance and resentment between workers that is sure to curtail respect and fuel friction.

Destroys Morale: Arrogant managers usually demonstrate an appalling lack of concern for subordinates. They commonly ignore input, and talk down to employees with condescending and sarcastic remarks. Rolling the eyes, making faces, scorn, and flaunting disgust are tactics used to browbeat and affect the actions of subordinates. Insults, mocking, and belittling are customary when the arrogant disagree with what is being said.

The toxic arrogant want to ensure that subordinates understand who owns dominance and clout. Both overtly and covertly, they want to convey the message that employees are "lucky to have a job." The obvious implication that accompanies this attitude is that the toxic have the power to hurt one's career or end the target's employment. No one likes to be looked down upon, or treated as though they are subhuman. Resentment is guaranteed, and inspiration to produce at the highest level is curtailed when employees feel like they are not valued team members.

Insist on Blind Loyalty: Toxic arrogant managers tend to be elitist. We will almost always find that they are consumed by their own self-importance and conceit. The arrogant truly believe that they are always right, that those around them are not as smart, and that the performance of others fails to meet their standard. Since they think that they know the answer to everything, the persona of the toxic arrogant is usually autocratic. Do not be surprised when the arrogant takes credit for every success.

Exaggerating their own self-worth makes it highly likely that the toxic arrogant will insist on blind loyalty from direct reports. The problem is that the arrogant expect devotion to them as a person because of their obvious greatness. Unsighted allegiance to an individual because that person sees themselves as exceptional is a perversion to the concept of mission loyalty. What the toxic manager is really seeking is much more like obedience, capitulation, and adulation.

Longer term damage: The elitism of the toxic arrogant runs the risk of establishing a workplace culture of unpleasantness. Meanness and ill-treatment produces ire and bitterness. An angry workforce increases conflict, mistrust, and hostility. Contemptuous behavior may lead to emotional injury, physical injury, or suicide. The more egregious scenarios end with arguments, name-calling, threats, or battery. The severity of the dispute could facilitate unwanted publicity, incarceration of employees, and financial instability.

Employees who are demeaned may lose devotion for their employer. In the case of a toxic arrogant boss, unhappy employees often try to escape the despondency of their situation. Instability will worsen as many will attempt to gain transfers or leave the organization altogether. Lost time from work, stress, anxiety, sleep disturbance, and depression can all amplify as workers suffer and seek relief.

15 Ways to Know A Toxic Indecisive Boss When You See One

Hesitant decision-maker / everything is tentative

Like to wait and see if more information will develop

Prefers guidance and instruction from superiors before they proceed

Blind follower - whatever executives say is the gospel

Black hole manager / proposals get lost or buried on their desk

Never willing to ruffle feathers of administration

Overly conservative, safe, and predictable if they do make a decision

Timid

Reluctant to confront poor performance

Takes great pride in viewing themselves as the supervisors ultimate team player

If questioned by administrators, they go into crisis mode and rework must be done immediately

Requires direct reports to tell them everything and get approval prior to taking action

Struggles internally with a lack of confidence in themselves

Often give answers that are safe and unobjectionable

Afraid of being innovative or trying new techniques

Chapter 7

TOXICITY OF INDECISIVENESS

Working for an indecisive supervisor is discouraging and demoralizing for employees. The classic "black hole" manager is sure to escalate the frustration level of your star performers to the point that they are likely to stop making suggestions for improvement. Those who just can't seem to pull the trigger are often trying to please everyone. Failing to take a stand on an important issue will cause the toxic boss to lose credibility amongst the people. Famed football coach Vince Lombardi said it best when he said, "Confidence is contagious; so is lack of confidence."

Anxiety over making a "wrong" decision can create delays, damage trust, and paralyze a team. The fear of failure often causes toxic indecisive managers to become overly conservative. There is a huge difference between playing to prevent losing, versus competing to win. Excessive caution, epitomized by a coach who is "playing not to lose" often ends up being very costly.

An example of playing not to lose involves a sports team that has a comfortable lead going into the fourth quarter. The coaches make a strategic end-of-game decision to play it safe, stall, or run out the clock. The oxymoron for the "slow it down and be careful" method of operation is that the strategy often fails. The team that was behind almost always makes a comeback, and frequently wins the game by snatching victory from the jaws of defeat.

Management indecisiveness is much like playing not to lose. Overreliance upon the "middle-of-the-road" style of direction leads to U- turns and outcome reversals. Start and stop; change, change, change, decision making discourages and deters the team.

Disheartened ineffectualness and impediment become standard operating procedure.

An additional problem for this method of operation is that many of law enforcement's most serious predicaments involve enormous doses of immediacy and consequence. Toxic indecisive bosses tend to become unnerved or flustered when faced with looming crisis. Decision-making paralysis in the public safety world can often have dangerous life and death implications. A decision-maker who can't muster the courage to "pull the trigger" when appropriate becomes a huge safety liability.

The stories that follow are just a few examples of inappropriate conduct by toxic indecisive bosses that far too many of us have witnessed throughout our careers.

Wait Until I Get There!

Uniform officers in a large police department were responding to a call about a suicidal female threatening to shoot herself. An on-duty uniform Sergeant marked in route to the call, but indicated that he was responding from a distance. After a couple of minutes, the Sergeant, who was still responding, requested an update from the officers who had just arrived on scene. The officers informed the Sergeant that they were outside with the husband and that no-one else was in the house with his wife. Additionally, communications indicated to the Sergeant that the female was on the phone with dispatch and was telling them she was going to shoot herself.

The door was locked and the husband did not have a key. The husband verbally gave permission for the officers to force entry into the home in order to help his wife. The Sergeant asked the officers on scene if they could safely get into a position that allowed them a clear view of the female and the surrounding area in the house. One officer covering the back of the residence stated he had a clear view of the residence and the female ranting on the phone. He advised he did not see any weapons in plain view. The Sergeant instructed the officers to take advantage of the current situation and force entry while the female was preoccupied on the phone.

The Shift Commander, a Lieutenant, emphatically stated over the air, "Negative, wait till I get there." The Sergeant arrived on scene and found that the female was now off the phone and not in view. The Sergeant made radio contact with the Lieutenant, advising that he was making a forced entry. The Lieutenant stated over the radio to the Sergeant, "Do not initiate forced entry" indicating that she, the boss, "Was not comfortable with kicking the door in."

The Sergeant asked communications to try and make contact with the female again. Luckily, she answered the phone and was again in view of the officer in the rear of the residence. In defiance of the verbal directive, the on-scene Sergeant took out a credit card and opened the door lock. Two officers and the Sergeant rushed the female and had her under control before she was able to get off the phone.

- *If you were the Sergeant in this situation, would you have given authorization for your officers to make entry, even though you were not yet on scene?*

- *How would you have responded when the Lieutenant provided clear direction over the radio that no forced entry was to take place until she arrived on scene?*

- *Would you have immediately forced entry into the home in deliberate violation of the directive from your supervisor?*

- *Should the Sergeant and/or the on-scene officers face disciplinary action?*

What the Hell is Wrong With You?

A Sergeant in a large sheriff's department was assigned to investigate a complaint from a citizen. Upon completion of her investigation, the Sergeant determined that the allegation was accurate and the complaint disposition was founded. The Sergeant completed her report, recommended discipline against the officer, and submitted the case file through the chain of command for review and approval.

Three days later the Sergeant and her supervisor were called to a meeting with their Division Commander. The Division Commander began the meeting by saying "What the hell is wrong with you" to the Sergeant. When the Sergeant asked for explanation, the Division Commander picked the Internal Affairs folder up off of his desk and proceeded to rip apart the quality of the report. The Division Commander cited three specific items that were omitted from the report. The Commander told the Sergeant that items one, two, and three must be inserted into the document for it to be complete. The Division Commander then threw the folder at the Sergeant, told her to make the corrections, and told her to resubmit the document within the hour.

At the conclusion of the meeting with the Division Commander, the puzzled Sergeant asked for a consultation with her supervisor. The Lieutenant told the Sergeant to make the corrections to the report as directed by the Division Commander. The Sergeant did as ordered and resubmitted the report.

One week later, the Sergeant was called to a meeting in the office of the Internal Affairs (IA) Commander. When the Sergeant responded to the Internal Affairs office, the IA Inspector began the meeting by saying "What the hell is wrong with you?" When the Sergeant asked for explanation, the IA Inspector told the Sergeant that her report was unacceptable. The IA Inspector told the Sergeant that she had to remove three items from the report before it would be considered complete and appropriate.

Yes, the items ordered removed by IA were the exact same three items that the Division Commander had ordered inserted into the report. The exasperated Sergeant threw her hands into the air thinking "what the hell is wrong with THEM?"

- *What conversation, if any, would you have had with the Division Commander who was ripping apart your report?*

- *What would you have done when your supervisor dismissed your concerns and told you to submit an incorrect report precisely as the Uniform Commander had directed?*

- *What conversation, if any, would you have had with the Internal Affairs Division Commander as he was ripping apart your amended report?*

Good Job, Uh, I Meant Not Such a Good Job

An experienced midnight shift officer was the DUI arrest king in his agency. The number of "under the influence" arrest and convictions that this officer attained far exceeded those of his peers. The king was recognized statewide as an expert in the art of detecting intoxication.

The agency that the DUI king worked for was considering the purchase of in-car video camera's for use on patrol. The department obtained a video cam and installed it in the DUI king's car to test it before they made the decision to purchase. One night shortly thereafter, the DUI king got into a vehicle pursuit with a suspected DUI driver. The vehicle pursuit lasted approximately 15 minutes, entered two different jurisdictions, and ultimately ended with a crash and an apprehension.

The DUI king's supervisor reviewed audiotape and (now that it was available) videotape as part of his supervisory review. The supervisor and several other high ranking officials were impressed with the videotape evidence and the performance of the officer. The supervisor issued a glowing commendation letter to the officer praising his performance.

Several days went by as the commendation letter and videotape were working their way up the chain of command. A high-ranking official who was reviewing the video of the pursuit decided that the tape contained evidence of the officer's poor performance during the chase. After consulting with a like-minded jurisdictional attorney about civil liability concerns, the high-ranking official insisted that the DUI king be written up for poor performance.

The supervisor, who had issued the glowing commendation letter to the officer, now issued him a disciplinary write-up form for the same incident.

- *Since you are recognized statewide as an expert in the detection of DUI offenders would you have questioned the high-ranking official's assessment of your judgment?*

- *How would you have responded when your supervisor subsequently issued a disciplinary action against you for the exact same incident that he had previously documented as praiseworthy performance?*

- *During your next pursuit, would you have found a way to ensure that the experimental video camera in your vehicle was not operable?*

- *What effect does this type of indecisive management have upon your future performance?*

Effect of Toxic Indecisive Manager on the Work Environment

Dictionary.com . . . defines indecisiveness as *vacillating, hesitant, or wavering.*

The following items will help us understand the devastating impact left in the wake of toxic indecisive managers.

Play-it-safe work environment: The toxic indecisive likes to play it safe and bask in the warm contentment of security. For this reason, they are very uncomfortable in a rapidly changing, high risk, fast-pace environment like law enforcement. Most commonly they will make statements such as, "Let me check with the boss before you take action on that," "Keep me informed," or "Let's wait and see what is going to happen." The toxic indecisive struggle with achieving measureable results, projects are frequently stalled, and proposals tend to get lost or buried on their desk.

Often timid and reluctant to confront poor performance, the toxic indecisive will commonly give safe, politically correct, or unobjectionable answers to queries. Cautious and tentative, when they do make a decision, they tend to be conformist and risk averse. It can be reasonably argued that the toxic indecisive boss is the worst cultural fit, and therefore the most dangerous of all law enforcement managers.

Paralysis by analysis: Toxic indecisive managers tend to overanalyze everything. Back and forth, back and forth, their internal struggle is colossal. It is hard to imagine how exhausting it must be to experience the inner turmoil of a decision-making wrestling match that never ends. The indecisiveness leads to a judicious modus operandi illustrated by hedging or dodging decision-making until they can get a feel for how the wind is blowing with superior officers.

Extreme procrastination toward taking action can cause the toxic to get hung up in fretting over all of the reasons not to move forward with a decision or a project. It is not uncommon for the indecisive to institute formal guidelines that prohibit direct reports from engagement until the supervisor either gets on scene or preemptively blesses an innocuous plan of action. Since toxic indecisive managers are slow to try new concepts, they frequently fail to present proposals up the chain of command. Newfangled ideas tend to die harmlessly on the vine.

Astonishing teammate: The toxic indecisive view themselves as the ultimate team player. After all, they are obedient, submissive, and would never question anything by management. In their mind, lack of confrontation, whether appropriate conflict or not, will make them look good to the boss. This type of manager sees themselves as a good soldier and strong partner with administration.

Indecisive supervisors and managers are very accommodating; they will do and say anything to prevent rocking the boat or angering executives. Though they may feel some remorse about it, the toxic indecisive will sacrifice direct reports to maintain a calm, uneventful status quo. If this type of manager works for a similarly toxic boss in their chain of command, the administrator will likely see the toxic indecisive in a very positive light. The irony of this phenomenon is that direct reports and anyone who is not toxic will view this type of manager as a dangerous roadblock who places subordinates at high risk of injury or death.

Long-term damage: Toxic indecisiveness creates misunderstanding and hesitancy amongst co-workers. Everyone understands that whatever direction has been provided by supervision is highly likely to change. Flip flop decision-making equates to frequent directional adjustment and much wasted time, as employees become masters of rework. Workers may develop a "what's the use" mindset upon acceptance that their creativity, productivity, teamwork, synergy, and collaboration are being muffled. Personnel who tend to throw their hands up, or shrug their shoulders while reciting something similar to "whatever you say" or "whatever you want to do boss" are a sure sign of indecisive management in the workplace.

Indecisive managers destroy morale. Victims are highly exasperated. Inspiration and enthusiasm of direct reports is devastated by a steady diet of politically correct statements and behaviors. "Don't do anything until I get there" supervision models bad behavior and makes it appear to followers that benign decision-making equates to success in the organization. Employee turnover and absenteeism are likely to increase as victims seek relief or freedom. Stress, anxiety, sleep disturbance, and depression can all amplify employee medical problems as workers suffer.

15 Ways to Know A Toxic Incompetent Boss When You See One

Relies heavily on politics and personal connections

Tells management what they want to hear

Overcompensate for their deficiencies – try too hard to project strength and confidence that direct reports see right thru

Excessively process oriented

Frequently request detailed reports and updates

Excessive use of charts, graphs and numeric measurement to demonstrate job performance

Struggles with spur of the moment decision-making

Fails to see the big picture

Makes bad decisions

Freezes, falls apart, or overreacts when faced with emergency

Uses confusing language – talks in circles, uses big words

Desperate to conceal ineptitude from superiors

Tamps down the creativity of direct reports to prevent subordinates from appearing more competent than them

Deceives management by projecting image that everything is under control

Lacks confidence in themselves as well as their direct reports

Chapter 8

TOXICITY OF INCOMPETENCY

The toxic incompetent manager is a principal of tomfoolery. Top brass usually views the incompetent performer favorably, yet everybody that works for the inept person understands that the toxic blunderer can't find their way out of a wet paper sack. Direct reports will unanimously testify that the incompetent supervisor doesn't have a clue as to what is really going on. Yet, despite poor performance, incapable bosses not only succeed in retaining their positions, often the bungling manager gets promoted again and again.

How is it that the executive viewpoint of the ineffectual manager is so diametrically different from how the same person is viewed by the average worker? Cagey executives should be able to spot this toxic loser right off of the bat. If executives would bother to listen to what the majority of their employees were saying, they would hear things such as "she is an idiot, how in the world did she get promoted," or "he is in way over his head." Sentiments such as "she has never accomplished anything in this business" and "how in the world could anybody expect him to be any good at managing a job that he could never do himself" are raging throughout the workplace.

But, alas, it all falls on deaf ears when it comes to the administrators. The toxic incompetent survives and thrives because they are masters of deception. The veneer that the incompetent supervisor presents to his or her boss is one of magical brilliance. They have learned to mask their deficiencies by presenting a carefully constructed image of themselves as they want to be seen. Desperate to conceal their ineptitude, the incompetent will rely on cronyism and friendships, rather than qualifications and proficiencies.

The mere fact that incompetents make bad decisions that prove to be wrong more often than they are right, is a significant problem for any organization. The decline of quality in organizational performance is obvious, but the trouble runs much deeper. Employees see right through the anemic boss, and when the boss has no credibility, effective leadership is next to impossible. The entire operation sputters and stumbles its way straight toward uselessness.

The stories that follow are just a few examples of inappropriate conduct by toxic incompetent bosses that far too many of us have witnessed throughout our careers.

We Just Did Not Have Enough to Hold Him!

A speeding vehicle roars by a uniform police officer who is working the overnight shift. The officer makes a U-turn to get behind the offender, and initiates a stop for the traffic violation. The driver, the only occupant of the vehicle, is very nervous, providing short yes or no answers to the officer's questions. The driver of the vehicle is not wearing trousers, and the Uniform officer observes reddish stains on the driver's shirt. Dirty boots with stains on them, and a bloody shovel are seen in plain view in the back seat.

The officer who made the stop was new to the profession. His gut instincts told him that further investigation was needed, so he requested help from a supervisor. When the Sergeant arrived on scene and began to interrogate the vehicle driver, additional information started to reveal itself. The vehicle driver indicated that an unknown suspect had attempted to rob him in an adjacent jurisdiction. The driver disclosed that he had struggled with the robber, that he struck the robber with the shovel, and that there was a possibility that the robbery suspect was dead. The vehicle driver then told officers that he was unable to pinpoint the location of where the alleged robbery and possible homicide had taken place.

By this time a Lieutenant had assumed command of the scene. The Lieutenant initiated basic investigative procedures. Officers found that no warrants existed for the driver. They then checked call logs in both jurisdictions and found no calls that would match circumstances as described by the driver. Approximately one hour had passed since the initial traffic stop. The Lieutenant began to worry that police had detained the driver for an excessive amount of time and ordered his immediate release. Thus a bloody driver with an unverifiable story, no pants on, and an admission that he may have killed someone with a shovel, is cut loose and sent on his way.

A very short time after the release of the bloody driver, a BOLO was received from an adjacent County for the vehicle and driver regarding a homicide that had occurred in their jurisdiction. Investigators from both agencies compared notes and attempted to relocate the suspect. Approximately four hours after the initial traffic stop, a different uniformed officer located and attempted to stop the suspect for a second time. A vehicle pursuit ensues. The same Lieutenant, who ordered the release of the suspect the first time, terminates the pursuit. The Lieutenant later opined that the high speeds and reckless behavior of the driver needlessly put the lives of innocent schoolchildren at risk as they waited at their school bus stops.

- *You are the Lieutenant described above. How long would you continue to detain the person of interest who was stopped for a traffic offense?*

- *Is the prolonged stop of the original traffic violator a detention, or should it be considered a custodial arrest?*

- *At what point and under what circumstances could a detention transform into an unintentional arrest?*

- *After a different officer got behind the now known murder suspect later that morning, would you have allowed the dangerous pursuit to continue?*

BOLO, Armed and Disgruntled

A federal law enforcement agency publicly issued a "BOLO" bulletin for one of their own agents who was under investigation for allegedly making threats. The bulletin advised both federal and regional law enforcement to be on the lookout for an agent who had expressed discord and made indirect threats to several different agency members. The BOLO told police that "She has threatened to show up at the headquarters office, though she no longer has access to the building." The BOLO further indicated that the agent was disgruntled and armed.

Problem is that the BOLO was issued publicly almost two-weeks after the Feds had already located and talked to the agent. In a news interview the agent's attorney stated, "The agent's location has been known to the Feds every day, and they are fully aware that she also is still in possession of her duty weapon and personally owned_weapons including an AR-15 registered with the federal government."

The agent, when reached at her home said, "I am not in hiding or on the run." The agent indicated that she was being retaliated against for complaints after being denied timely treatment after she suffered an injury. Her attorney indicated that the agent had faced previous acts of retaliation for numerous complaints lodged against supervisors over several years.

When the national news media asked why the bulletin, dated one week earlier, was distributed to law enforcement agencies after the agent had already been located, a spokesman said he had "no clue" and that it was "probably done in error."

- *What motivated this federal agency to issue a BOLO for one of their agents?*

- *What caused this BOLO to be distributed regionally two-weeks after the agency had already talked with its employee?*

- *If the agency was indeed investigating a personnel matter against one of their own, is it appropriate for*

them to share and distribute very personal informa-
tion regarding one of their employees?

- *The involved agent's attorney indicated that the agent*
  had made previous complaints against her employer.
  What role, if any, did retaliation play in the way this
  incident transpired?

Illegal Search and Pre-text
Drug Arrests

A veteran officer moved to a new county and started working for a large suburban police department. The veteran officer immediately approached his Sergeant and asked the supervisor about
performance expectations. The Sergeant tells the officer "Just go
out and do your job."

The veteran officer was proactive and made a drug arrest nearly every day. Approximately eight-months into his career
with the new department, the Sergeant wrote a disciplinary action
against the veteran for making illegal searches. The Sergeant had
reviewed every drug arrest and cited that the veteran officer had
used vehicle stops and traffic offenses as pretexts for making drug
arrests without consent or a warrant. The veteran officer attempted to show the Sergeant "State Code" that permitted inventory
searches, drug seizures, and resultant drug arrests, but the Sergeant
disagreed. The officer appealed the disciplinary action to the Lieutenant who ripped the document up and made the discipline that
the Sergeant dished out disappear.

Three months after the illegal search debacle, the veteran
transfer officer received his annual performance appraisal. The
same Sergeant ripped the officer and lowered the evaluation score
because "the veteran had not been recording keep checks, business
checks, or neighborhood checks on his mobile data terminal." The
veteran officer objected, stating that he had been conducting the
checks, but that he was not aware that he was expected to play the
numbers game with his computer. The Sergeant's response was "I
shouldn't have to spoon-feed you on how to do your job."

- *What responsibility does an officer have regarding the clarity of his or her own performance expectations?*

- *How would you have responded when your supervisor issued a disciplinary action against you for allegedly conducting illegal searches and seizures?*

- *How would you have responded when your supervisor lowered your performance appraisal rating for alleged failures with which you disagree?*

- *How would you have responded if the next level in your chain of command upheld the actions of the Sergeant?*

<u>Negative Effects of Toxic Incompetency on the Workplace</u>

Dictionary.com . . . defines incompetency as *lacking qualification or ability; incapable.*

The work that follows is an attempt to explain some of the more significant long-term damage caused by toxic incompetents.

Make me look good work environment: When toxic incompetent supervisors understand that their skill level is substandard, they will frequently restrict the independence and freedom of their direct reports. This tactic is designed to "keep things from getting out of hand" by eliminating virtually all risk. Direct reports are told what to do, how to do it, and when the task should be completed. The incompetent often feel that if they severely constrict activity under their watch, nothing damaging will transpire. If negative events do not occur, then the incompetent achieve their goal of looking like a good manager in the eyes of those who are powerful in the agency.

Toxic incompetent supervisors who do not understand that their skill level is substandard usually try to influence others by overcompensating for their weaknesses. Bragging, being a blowhard, or trying too hard to fake expertise is an attempt to hoodwink their audience. Often time's toxic incompetents also need to continually reinforce to themselves that they have skills. Political affiliations become a top priority. A lot of time is spent kissing the backside of people that incompetents think they need to bamboozle so that they can help them attain their next goal.

That is the way they want it done: Incompetent managers try to follow policy and procedure to the letter, no exceptions. Over reliance on policy and procedure causes the toxic incompetent to believe that they are covered or absolved of responsibility so long as everything was done by the book. Since lack of skill and proficiency keeps them from understanding the big picture, incompetent's implement straight arrow management to ensure that they will be viewed as "on board" and always on the same side of the issue as the boss.

Incompetent supervisors fear being unmasked. They try desperately to stay in the boss's good graces at any cost so that their personal deficiencies will not be exposed. It is not unusual for this type of manager to tamp down on the ability of direct reports. They theorize that close control over the activities of star performers can keep the star from outshining them; the toxic bosses. Under-my-thumb management is an attempt to prevent exposure of the bosses' incompetency. Agreeableness, dullness, and compliance help facilitate the uncanny ability of these underachievers to hold onto their positions despite their obvious failings.

Cronyism and Statistics: Toxic incompetent managers rely primarily upon cronyism to survive and prosper. They must use compliments, accolades, and brownnosing to sway their image with the bosses. Cultivating a close personal friendship is one way of successfully manipulating what the manager's might see in their mind's eye when they observe the employees. Heartfelt personal bonds, or a fondness for someone, make it much more likely that the executive viewpoint will be skewed affirmatively during the course of evaluation for the incompetent.

Toxic incompetents are likely to be much more process focused managers than people oriented leaders. They waste an enormous amount of time trying to prove their own worthiness by using numbers, charts, graphs, and statistical data. Of course, they must require direct reports to collect and submit large amounts of data to feed the stat monster. Since the incompetents do not have much luck getting the job done in the field, they tend to overindulge in controlling the message to management.

Enduring damage: Toxic incompetent managers have a tendency to make poor choices and bad decisions. Many times their directives make no sense at all, and if followed would lead to disaster and/or civil liability. This puts workers in the unenviable position of ignoring the idiotic directive and taking contrary action just to get the job done. Going against a supervisory directive puts both the employees and the agency in a potentially litigious situation.

If they do not have an opportunity to confer with their boss, the incompetents will usually make miscalculated decisions that ultimately obliterates morale and motivation. Though the toxic incompetents do not know any better, the ineptness of their management causes much frustration and angst for the workers. Since most employees are indeed striving toward excellence, the association with poor quality outputs can impact attitude and devastate motivation.

Personal shortcomings prohibit the unqualified from recognizing exceptional endeavors. The incompetent simply do not possess the capacity to recognize individual brilliance or superior performance. They have no idea what talent looks like because their own field of vision limits their viewpoint. Therefore, the incompetent will not and likely cannot recognize or promote exceptional achievement amongst direct reports.

15 Ways to Know A Toxic Micromanager When You See One

Control freak

Imposes ridiculous artificial deadlines

Feels a neurotic need to make decisions and over manage

Fanatical about time management

Highly critical

Heavy handed supervision and willing to sacrifice subordinates

Phobic in their attempt to control risk

Compulsively requests detailed status updates

Disproportionate use of charts, graphs and measurement techniques

Excessively process oriented

Monitors tasks obsessively

Finds comfort when they have instant access to facts that back up their position

Likes to take credit for success and shift blame to others

Eager to manipulate their image so as not to look foolish to superiors

Rewarded by management for attention to detail and having their act together

Chapter 9

TOXICITY of MICROMANAGEMENT

Great leaders set their employees up for success. Toxic micromanagement is the opposite of good leadership. The toxic boss restricts the ability of micromanaged people to develop and grow. It limits what the micromanager's team can achieve, because every action must be approved and sanctioned by the supervisor. Toxic micromanagers typically turn even the most simple tasks or assignments into laborious chores.

Excessive scrutiny destroys confidence, initiative and motivation. Russian-American novelist, philosopher, playwright, and screenwriter Ayn Rand said, "The quickest way to kill the human spirit is to ask someone to do mediocre work."

The toxic micromanager is obsessed with control. Fear of failure is the driving force in their world. They worry that unless they regulate every aspect of the environment, their domain could be destroyed. Micromanagers in law enforcement are so process-oriented that they often overwhelm the average officer with heaps of useless drudgery and documentation. Their need to make most decisions and to monitor tasks obsessively encourages sheep-like behavior from subordinates.

Toxic micromanagers seldom praise and often criticize. They commonly reject reports or projects, insisting on small meaningless revisions. Red pens, strikethroughs, and wording amendments send a clear message that the work of the underling is not acceptable. In reality the noted corrections are typically insignificant, but the impact on the subordinate is a lesson that nothing seems good enough. Frustrated and beaten down, victims of the micromanager will learn to work to minimum standards and often wonder why the manager doesn't just do it themselves.

The stories that follow are just a few examples of inappropriate conduct by toxic micromanager bosses that far too many of us have witnessed throughout our careers.

Give Me Your Badge and Gun

A young inexperienced police officer and a senior officer respond to a call for service. The two officers were questioning the caller and attempting to determine the facts and circumstances behind the request for service. When the Sergeant arrived on-scene, he was monitoring the state of affairs and assessing potential services.

The more experienced officer decided that he was no longer needed on the call and exits the apartment. As the veteran officer is preparing to leave the scene and make himself available for other calls, he is followed outside and stopped in the yard by the Sergeant. The Sergeant, obviously very angry, begins to yell at the veteran officer, stating that he (supervisor) is holding the veteran officer accountable for mistakes made at the scene of the call. The irate Sergeant, in a derogatory and demeaning tone, tells the veteran officer that he is expected to take charge of a scene, and that the senior officer is going to be held personally accountable for the perceived failings of the younger officer.

The veteran officer is resentful and shocked by the tone and nature of the supervisor's behavior. The veteran officer is also unhappy that the ugly confrontation is taking place in a public place in full view of several spectators. The senior officer states, "I do not have to take abuse like that, especially in public." The veteran officer turns to walk away. The Sergeant becomes more enraged, emphatically screaming an ultimatum, telling the senior officer to return for further discussion or face immediate suspension.

The senior officer decided that it was best to attempt to deescalate the encounter. He silently started walking toward his automobile. The Sergeant, in the parking lot of the apartment complex demands the officer's badge and gun shouting, "You are suspended from duty for insubordination!" The veteran officer removes his badge from his uniform shirt, gives the Sergeant his gun, and drives away from the scene.

Approximately thirty minutes later, the supervisor instructs the senior officer to meet with him at the precinct building. The Sergeant returned the veteran's badge and gun, telling him to get back to work.

- *If you were the veteran officer described above, how would you have responded when the Sergeant angrily confronted you in a public parking lot with witnesses present?*

- *Regarding the initial outdoor confrontation, would you consider the actions of the veteran officer insubordinate?*

- *If you were the veteran officer, how would you have responded when the Sergeant demanded your badge and gun?*

- *If you were the veteran officer, how would you have responded when the Sergeant told you to forget that the incident ever happened and return to duty?*

Sergeant is All Over the Radio

Uniform officers were responding to a call involving an armed robbery at an indoor flea market. Information provided by communications was that numerous young adults had entered into the flea market and assaulted and robbed the janitor. While the officers were responding, a Police Sergeant is on the radio barking out orders as to how he wants the officers to perform. The orders relayed by the Sergeant are "elementary," basic procedures that the officers already perform routinely.

Upon arrival, officers set up a perimeter and arrest several suspects. Officers were still looking for one additional suspect. The Sergeant continues to be all over the radio, micromanaging every-one with extraordinarily basic commands such as "do not let the suspects talk, keep them in separate cars, and preserve evidence at the scene."

While searching a tractor trailer yard just north of the flea market, officers noticed a car parked nose end up against a trailer. Investigation indicated that the vehicle was registered in a city approximately 100 miles away, the hood was cold, and it looked like the vehicle had been sitting there for quite a while. The officers determine that the vehicle had no connection to the robbery.

The voracious "know it all" Sergeant heard the officers run the car's license tag and responded over to the location. The Sergeant felt certain that the car had something to do with the call. The Sergeant pulled out a slim Jim and broke into the car. He searched the whole car and found a pair of bolt cutters in the back seat. As the Sergeant continued to search the vehicle, another officer was able to make contact with a driver who worked for the tractor trailer company. This driver confirmed that the vehicle belonged to one of their employees and that the vehicle had no connection to the robbery.

- *What are the short-and long-term effects of the Sergeants verbalization of elementary orders to responding officers?*

- *What are the short-and long-term effects of the Sergeants domination of the radio airways?*

- *How would you have responded when the Sergeant illegally entered and illegally searched a vehicle that belonged to an innocent party?*

- *How did the on-scene behavior of the Sergeant impact the search for the suspect that was still at large?*

<u>I'm Telling you Who Will be the Nominee</u>

A police commander is charged with the responsibility of annually identifying the agency "Employee of the Year." The procedure for making this determination was clearly spelled out by departmental policy.

The commander following department policy, convened a panel and identified a nominee. The commander met with the Chief of Police to advise him of the choice. The Chief of Police immediately rejected the nomination and told the commander who he (Chief) had identified as his choice to win the award.

The commander reminded the Chief that the selection had been made according to policy. The Chief of Police ordered the commander to reconvene the panel and undertake a second vote. The commander reluctantly complied as ordered and reconvened the panel. The panel voted a second time for the original nominee, offering no change to their original decision.

The commander once again met with the Chief and told him of the panel's nominee. The Chief was boiling point furious and began to yell at the commander, calling him defiant and disloyal. The Chief ordered the commander to resubmit the nomination in memo format with the name of the Chiefs candidate listed as the nominee.

Though the commander was very uncomfortable with the process, he submitted the memo as directed by the Chief. However, the memo detailed a description of the entire set of events including the fact the Chief had dictated who was going to be the award winner. Upon reading the memo, the Chief unceremoniously blew his stack! The Chief of Police angrily said things such as, "You are not a team player," "I'll get your job," and "You're an insubordinate   f *#@!!%" before ordering the commander to leave the office.

- *How would you have responded when the Chief rejected the process as dictated by policy and revealed his choice of who was going to win the prestigious annual award?*

- *Would you have complied with the Chief's order to convene the panel a second time even though you knew that the results desired by the boss were predetermined?*

- *When questioned by the reconvening panel, what would you tell them about the need for a second vote?*

- *How would you respond when the Chief of Police called you demeaning names and threatened to see that you would be fired from your job?*

Negative Effects of Micromanager on the Workplace

Dictionary.com . . . defines micromanagement as *to manage or control with excessive attention to details.*

The following section will help us understand the damaging consequences that the micromanager dispenses upon those in their office sector.

Oppressive and overregulated workplace: The toxic micromanager creates a work environment that is loaded with processes, restrictions, and regulations. Workers must conform to the bosses many personal rules, and perform as directed with excessive adherence to "by the book" behaviors. Creativity, independence, and freedom are restrained as workers are told what to do, how to do it, and when task completion is expected. Micromanagers are more often than not schedule and time-management maniacs who have little tolerance for those who do not share their obsession.

Control freaks: The toxic micromanager is likely to be a perfectionist and workaholic. They over plan, and commonly set unworkable or impractical deadlines for assignments. The toxic micromanager will delegate responsibility but not authority. Employees are effectively neutered when left in a hopeless situation with little or no decision-making clout. Though the toxic are sometimes good at getting things accomplished, the toll that it takes upon staff is enormous.

The micromanager is addicted to the emotional state of mind that involves proving themselves, being in charge, and getting their way. The classic "my way or the highway" boss is the epitome of a sheep-in-wolves clothing supervisor. They like to present themselves as mild mannered and even handed, but they become vicious and vengeful behind closed doors if the tranquility of their world is circumvented. They will tear the sheep to shreds when it advances the restoration of order or makes them look good to superior officers.

Willing to do management's dirty work: Toxic micromanagers are ruthless rule enforcers who relentlessly pursue orderliness and procedures. They are likely to be harsh, unsympathetic, and unforgiving when interacting with direct reports. The toxic use annual performance appraisals as a means to admonish, censure, and reprimand those under their command. The focus of the review is almost always going to be on reaffirming perceived weaknesses, rather than on development of the employee.

Toxic micromanagers will set up win-lose scenarios between supervisor's, direct reports, and coworkers in their attempts to control and manipulate the working environment. Preferred tactics include nitpicking, hairsplitting, and fault-finding. Their appetite for being judgmental and highly critical is gluttonous because they insist on being right even at the expense of others. Toxic micromanagers actually relish the role of hangman because it helps them engineer and govern office affairs.

Lasting damage: Victims of the classic toxic micromanager may experience low self-esteem, feel paralyzed, powerless, and helpless. Oppressive mismanagement will extinguish optimism, and obliterate loyalty while simultaneously creating misunderstanding and hesitancy amongst coworkers. Workers may develop a "why waste my time, you are going to redo it anyway" mindset upon acceptance that their creativity, productivity, teamwork, synergy, and collaboration are being silenced.

Toxic micromanagers create unnecessary work and frustrate morale to no end. Victims are highly exasperated and understand that they will never be able to get anything right the first time. The continuous lack of faith in subordinates models bad behavior and makes it appear to followers that overregulation and demeaning conduct equates to success in the organization. Employee turnover and absenteeism are likely to increase as victims seek relief. Stress, anxiety, sleep disturbance, and depression can all amplify employee medical problems as workers agonize over their predicaments. Unhappy employees will try to flee the misery of their situation, and many will leave the organization altogether.

15 Ways to Know A Toxic Untruthful Boss When You See One

Good actors - charming and manipulative

Like to spin facts

Favorable documenters - will modify facts & figures

Defensive reaction if a lie is challenged

Expects that others will be untruthful

Masters of embellishment

Purposely misleads

Overemphasizes that they are telling the truth when telling a lie

Lies to ward off trouble

Quick to cover up

Concocts excuses

Frequently changes their story

Likes to rewrite history with their falsehoods

Suppresses facts

Fabricates accomplishments

Chapter 10

TOXICITY OF THE UNTRUTHFUL

All law enforcement agencies have robust policies that mandate truthfulness and prohibit dishonesty. In fact, pre-employment, the profession incorporates polygraph examinations and extensive background investigations to eliminate those who use their tongues to deceive. One of the first lessons taught to new hires in recruit school is to never tell a lie! Strong emphasis is placed upon the concept, "you can be forgiven for almost any mistake if you tell the truth, but if you lie you will be terminated." Integrity and truthfulness resonate to the core of many public safety professionals.

It would follow logically that a profession that values veracity to the degree found in law enforcement would be free of untruthfulness. Tasks such as maintaining the public trust, making arrests, obtaining search warrants, and testifying in court rely on integrity and truth telling. Most law enforcement officers personify high personal standards and perform righteously on a daily basis. The dangers caused by the toxic untruthful are incredibly acute, yet, straight talk demands that we acknowledge that there are substantial numbers of people in the public safety workplace that are known to be significant fabricators.

Plato once said "false words are not only evil in themselves, but they infect the soul with evil." The perplexing paradox for law enforcement is that many toxic managers often lead the misrepresentation trail by employing varying degrees of truth in the execution of their daily duties. Think about the modeled behavior that ranges from pathological lying, political deceit, lying for convenience, duplicity for personal gain, spinning the message, and dishonesty to cover your rear end. Far too many toxic managers wouldn't know the truth if it slapped them in the face.

Some "confirmed law enforcement falsifiers" at lower levels are banned from testifying in court or placed in non-critical functions. To the educated observer, this tactical decision looks like cutting-edge fool's gold. It would probably be just as effective to hang a sign around their neck that reads, "Liar, liar, pants on fire"! Whether they reside at the top or the bottom of the organization, modern-day public safety agencies must change their willingness to codify employees who are proven liars. When the bosses are hypocrites, the only way to accomplish a righteous mission is in spite of their so called leadership.

The stories that follow are just a few examples of inappropriate conduct by toxic untruthful bosses that far too many of us have witnessed throughout our careers.

Deputy Chief Caught Lying

A police officer is arrested for an alleged crime that is committed while the officer is off-duty and out of uniform. The officer is booked and his name and picture are provided to the news media by the agency.

The Chief of Police issues a statement to the media that says in essence, "This department has very high standards of integrity and we will not tolerate this type of behavior from one of our officers." As details of the incident and the investigation begins to leak out, overwhelmingly the department members are outraged over the poor investigation, the weak probable cause, and the lack of support shown to the accused officer.

Weeks go by with anger festering within the agency. Finally, the administration decided that the Deputy Chief of Police should attend some roll-call sessions to deflate rumors and dissent among the troops. At one particular roll-call session, a veteran officer asks the Deputy Chief why the department had considered the complainant's statements to be reliable when in fact the accusers had lied to investigators about their own significant criminal history. The veteran officer also asked the Deputy Chief why a prosecutor was not consulted prior to initiating a criminal charge against a police officer.

The Deputy Chief stopped the officer in mid-sentence, gave him an aggressive look and stated "I don't know where you are getting your information, but the victims have never been arrested, charged or convicted of any crime." The Deputy Chief went on to say "If you continue to talk about this case you will be subject to a subpoena because this is an ongoing investigation." The Deputy Chief ignored the question about consultation with the prosecutor, even though peer officers knew for a fact that a prosecutor was never approached by investigators prior to arrest of the accused officer.

A few weeks later numerous officers attend the probable cause hearing for their friend. Sure enough the bad guys had been arrested, charged and convicted of serious crimes. They had lied to the police during their recorded interview, and investigators had not discovered much of the damaging background data on the offenders prior to the arrest of the officer.

The criminal case against the arrested officer was ultimately dismissed in court.

- *Is an open forum the right place for a high-ranking official to be discussing an internal investigation?*

- *Were the veteran officer's sensitive questions to the Deputy Chief regarding an investigation of a peer officer appropriate?*

- *How would you have reacted when the Deputy Chief's comments became aggressive and threatening?*

- *How do you think the results of this open-forum exchange impacted the officers and the police organization?*

It Never Happened

The Chief of Police is unhappy with what he perceives as inappropriate performance by one of his commanders. The Chief begins to pick on every word and seeks ways to discredit the commander. The Chief has made public statements to the commander such as, "You're a screw-up," and, "I'm going to get you."

The Chief fails to attend the kick-off of a significant co-hosted training course. Once he realizes that he missed the kick-off, the Chief directs a Major to write-up the commander for failing to inform, and for failure to make sure the event was on the Chief's calendar.

A Major calls the commander to his office. The Major presents a document to the commander and directs him to read it and sign it. Even though no dates, times, or specific facts support the allegations, the document details in great length how the commander had consistently failed to notify the Chief of Police of significant departmental events.

The commander objected to the disciplinary action and stated emphatically that the allegations were not true. The commander insisted that he had in fact told the Chief about the single event in question, and that there had never been any accusations of this nature in the past. The Major and the commander disagree several times over the truthfulness of the accusations.

The Major orders the commander to sign the document and informs him that the document will be placed in the commander's personnel file as a disciplinary action. The commander signs the document as ordered. But, before he returned it to the Major, he also listed in detail on the form that the facts listed were fiction, total fabrication, and that a performance error never occurred.

- *What role, if any, did the Chief's positional influence over the Major play in this disciplinary write-up of the commander?*

- *If you were the commander in this situation, how would you respond to the demand that you sign and acknowledge a disciplinary form that erroneously detailed your poor performance?*

- *If you were the Major in this case, how would you have responded when the Chief insisted that you discipline the commander without factual justification?*

- *What conversation, if any, would you have with the Chief of Police following this incident?*

<u>*Our Chief Wouldn't Do That!*</u>

A citizen files a complaint against a police employee alleging excessive force during an arrest. The controversial complaint is investigated and a supervisor recommends that the complaint should be sustained against the officer and punishment assessed. The officer disagrees and appeals the decision through a resolution policy designated by the employer.

The second step in the appeals process involves a meeting with the Chief of Police. During this meeting, the Chief threatens the officer, telling him among other things, "I hold your career in my hands," and "If you know what is good for you, you will drop the appeal of this case and comply with the punishment."

The officer believes he is not guilty, so he tells the Chief that he wishes to continue his appeal to the next level (a meeting with the top Municipal Executive). The Chief becomes angry and issues direct threats toward the officer and his career. The officer secretly tape recorded his meeting with the Chief. The accused officer leaves the meeting with no favorable resolution to his concerns.

The accused officer then meets with the top Municipal Executive as Step 3 in the appeals process for this jurisdiction. The officer reveals to the top governmental official that the Police Chief was demeaning, and that he threatened to end or stymie the officer's career. The Executive official states "I have discussed this matter with the Chief, and our Chief would not do that. I am quite sure that the Chief of Police did not threaten your job." The officer is told that he "obviously misunderstood" the Chief's comments. The Municipal Executive and the head of HRM tell the officer that they are supporting the Chief's finding and upholding the discipline.

The accused officer indicates that he had not misunderstood the intentions of the Chief. The officer then produces and plays for the officials the previously recorded audiotape of his meeting with the Chief. The Executive and the head of HRM are visibly shaken when they hear the tape. It is obvious to everyone in the room that the Chief's statements and actions were clearly inappropriate. The high administrators ask the officer to turn over possession of the tape recording, which the officer refuses.

A few days later, the accused officer is notified that, effective immediately, he was exonerated of all internal charges and was to return to full duty. A few weeks after the incident, the accused officer is transferred to a highly desirable position within the agency.

- *Though legal in this state, is there an ethical dilemma created when the accused officer secretly tape recorded his private meeting with the Chief?*

- *Would the outcome of this disciplinary action have been different without the presence of a secret audiotape?*

- *The executive official initially supported the Chief and upheld the discipline against the accused officer. Was this support grounded in bias, blindness, ignorance, corruption, or some combination of all?*

- *Should the Chief of Police face disciplinary action even though he believed that his conversation with the accused officer was private and privileged?*

Business and Ethics Don't Go Together

Many public safety agencies are experiencing high turnover rates and are chronically understaffed. The Chief of Police makes it clear to the civilian personnel who are in charge of recruiting and hiring that the numbers must improve. The civilian supervisors feel significant pressure and begin to employ various methods including reduction of guidelines to meet perceived numerical hiring standards.

Recruiting personnel begin to aggressively pursue "previously-certified" officers. Pre-certs are fully trained officers currently employed by other police agencies. These officers are immediately available and require much less training than do new recruits.

This jurisdiction's recruiters implement a strategy designed to lure pre-cert officer to their agency by advocating improved benefits to perspective employees. Of particular focus is a promise that the jurisdiction seeking the pre-cert officer's services offers much better health care. A number of pre-cert officers are hired, all with the understanding that their health care benefit would be paid by the agency, even during retirement.

A few days after these officers are hired; the jurisdiction changes the health-care benefit plan considerably. None of the newly hired officers will have paid health care as promised under this new plan. The officers are outraged by the pre-hiring deception, and request a meeting with the hiring director. At this meeting, the hiring manager initially indicates that he had no knowledge that the benefit was about to be taken away. When pressed, the manager does admit that the benefit reduction discussion had been ongoing for at least two years, and stated "I am sorry, but sometimes business and ethics just do not go together."

- *The manager was under extreme administrative pressure to meet hiring quotas. What impact did this pressure have on his decision to omit possible benefit changes from discussions with recruits?*

- *If you were a new hire who had been deceived, how would you have responded when the Manager admitted benefit reduction discussions had been ongoing for at least two years?*

- *How would you have responded when the Manager stated that sometimes business and ethics do not go together?*

Effect of the Toxic Untruthful Manager in the Workplace

Dictionary.com . . . defines untruthful as *wanting in veracity; diverging from or contrary to the truth; not corresponding with fact or reality. A person who tells lies.*

Let's take a moment to examine some of the damage that is caused by the liar, liar, pants on fire manager.

Creates a duty to lie workplace: Truth be known, those entrusted with leadership and supervisory responsibilities are some of the worst Pinocchios' in the law enforcement profession. Many managers feel that the telling of lies is simply an acceptable cost of doing business. Regrettably, too many also believe that playing the game, or engaging in toxic untruthful behavior is necessary in order to survive and thrive in law enforcement.

Since privacy must not be breached, lying bosses often use the excuse of secrecy to cover their mistruths. Other toxic untruthful managers constantly slant the message to employees either "for their own good" or because "they don't need to know." Still others in authority are experts at lying by omission, or not telling the whole truth. And, CYA seems to be the quantitative king of workplace dishonesty when untruthfulness becomes a habit on the job.

Perversion of Integrity: The trust dynamic is applied consistently to both individuals and to their agencies. The toxic untruthful individual tries to impress or gain an advantage with their falsehoods. Deception causes the corrosion of worker integrity. The unhealthy erosion of innermost trust will ensure that personal and business reliability perishes. When even one officer loses their "good name" and reputation, ramifications are felt throughout the law enforcement profession.

When a law enforcement agency fails to deal effectively with one of the toxic untruthful, they do so at their own peril. Deceitfulness puts the individual and the agency on a slippery slope of vulnerability. Unimpeded lying can be invigorating to some, the more the liar gets away with the behavior the more they will use the ploy. Lies also tend to become bigger and bigger over time. If a liar has success in the workplace, others are more likely to employ the same tactics.

Creates a culture of mistrust and dysfunction: Of what a tangled web is weaved, when toxic managers practice to deceive. Dishonest management is reflective of a dysfunctional organizational culture. A mutual lack of respect and trust severely damages the vital working relationship between employees and management. Deceit, hypocrisy, and envy can cripple organizational morale. Employees lose faith in the institution. Those immersed in a fraudulent culture must ask themselves "is this an organization worthy of my loyalty and affiliation?"

The level of trust between the community and their public servants is directly proportional to the crime fighting success of the agency. Residents rely on equitable motives and behaviors to maintain the public confidence. Trust can take years to cultivate, yet literally be broken in the twinkling of an eye. Loss of credibility causes co-workers, customers, and supervisors to question motives and doubt reliability. A community that has lost faith in their officers no longer believes anything that comes from the deceivers.

Prolonged damage: Victims of an untruthful manager are very upset, angry, and disappointed. Verbal naughtiness produces a workforce full of discord, skepticism, and bitterness. Suspicion and mistrust will devastate optimism and inspiration. Spoken caginess can destroy reputations and alter the course or outcome of investigations and official proceedings. Turnover is likely to increase as despondent personnel try to abscond from the source of their distress.

Toxic untruthful managers lose respect. Victims are decidedly infuriated by the department's lack of action and accountability. The agency itself becomes immoral when dishonest conduct becomes systematic. Individuals whose personal moral code is in conflict with agency values will at best be less productive and emotionally detached. Steady and continuous immoral activities by leaders models bad behavior, and make it appear to followers that dishonesty and lying equate to success in the organization. Stress,

anxiety, and depression can all amplify employee medical problems as workers agonize over their predicaments.

15 Ways to Know A Toxic Corrupt Boss When You See One

Compulsive lying, cheating, and/or stealing

"If there is no law or policy against it," it is not forbidden

Little or no conscience

Possess elevated manipulation skills

Blurs the lines of truth

Trust in "no harm, no foul"

Ends justify the means belief system

Can't seem to resist prohibited opportunities

Stretches ethical boundaries

Takes advantage of loopholes

Personal value system is feeble and pliable

Criminal and policy violator

Hides illegitimate behavior

Willing to overlook the small stuff

Governed by justification mentality

Chapter 11

TOXICITY OF THE MORALLY BANKRUPT

Integrity is the cornerstone of the law enforcement vocation. The government grants enormous authority to policing with the expectation that the institution will respect the constitutional rights of people as to liberty, equality, and justice. Citizens voluntarily grant immense power to law enforcement largely on the basis of trust and service. Deviant, dishonest, improper, unethical, or criminal behavior bleeds the lifeblood out of the government, the people, and the law enforcement organization.

Misuse of police authority for personal gain, i.e. abuse of position or corruption, is a perversion of authority that violates the remarkable confidence invested in the profession. The level of misapplication and exploitation that exists is often the topic of great disagreement within the enforcement occupation. Whether criminal, intentional, without remorse, or whether it takes the form of satisfying desires for status and comfort, abuse and corruption subsidizes moral deterioration of the officer and of the agency.

Though the big picture effect is debatable, minor gratuities such as the free cup of coffee, professional courtesy, or a reduced price meal at the local diner, do not cause catastrophic ruin. The egregious nature of deliberate illicit activity, violence, and morally bankrupt supervision cultivates an assortment of dreadful consequences that end in devastation. Law enforcement leadership must not allow structural leniency nor systematic apathy to obliterate the entrustment contract between police and the community.

Organizational tolerance and deliberate indifference of the toxic and morally bankrupt agencies are primarily the providence of supervision and management. Whether a supervisor is permitting prejudices, animosities, or friendships to influence decision-making by accepting gratuities, or committing criminal acts, the exploitation, sleaze, and dishonesty of immorality in law enforcement distorts and destroys integrity. Compromised bosses who engage in scurrilous behavior, or who fail to make the difficult decisions that relate to subordinate misconduct, underwrite entity corrosion that if unhindered, will lead to atomic bomb like destruction.

The stories that follow are just a few examples of inappropriate conduct by toxic corrupt bosses that far too many of us have witnessed throughout our careers.

Domestic Terrorist

An on-duty federal law enforcement officer notices that 23 persons from special interest countries (high risk nations for potential terrorism) are allowed to enter the United States without following proper protocol. No documents were checked, and no fingerprints where run through any databases. The officer believed that the entries could be a significant breach of national security.

Per agency SOP, the officer reported the suspicious activity to a supervisor. The supervisor told the agent to report the information to the agency's intelligence section. It just so happened, that all Intel officers were off on the day in question, so the operation of the entire intelligence section was shut down. In good faith, the Federal officer reported his suspicions to a Joint Terrorism Task Force (JTTF) headed up by the Federal Bureau of Investigations (FBI).

The federal officer's supervisors were very unhappy that he made a report to a law enforcement agency outside their own. Over the course of the next few weeks and months, the officer's employer initiated a total of 19 internal investigations against him. The weight of the witch-hunt took its toll, and the officer eventually left the agency. In the end, a total of 54 internal investigations; including an allegation of being a domestic terrorist, were launched against the officer.

The officer in question filed an EEOC complaint against the agency regarding the circumstances surrounding the discontinued employment. The disposition of the complaint was favorable to the officer, as the ruling went against his Federal employer. Approximately 2-weeks after the EEOC ruling, the former officer's home was raided. The agent's former employer landed a helicopter in the officer's front yard, and armed officials in tactical gear forcibly entered the home.

Though no arrests were ever made, personal items were seized from her home, property was damaged, occupants were forcibly detained, and the officer ended up without a job in the career of his dreams. The officer was never charged with any crime.

- *Is it appropriate for an officer to report a suspicious incident to a different government entity outside of their own agency?*

- *Did a perceived lack of loyalty impact the agencies response to the actions of this employee?*

- *What do the 54 internal investigations and a subsequent tactical raid tell us about the management mindset at this agency?*

- *How would you have responded when your former employer raided your home in tactical gear and forcibly detained some of your relatives?*

Suspended for Lunch

A federal law enforcement supervisory officer had a reputation for "giving" seizures to certain of his favorite agents at the airport. Even when one officer would find the drugs, the supervisor would call someone else over to process the seizure. The favored officer would end up with his/her name on the computer reports. Credit for drug seizures are important, it meant award money at the end of the year, it has a bearing on promotions, and it even affects whether the officer involved moves to specialized enforcement teams.

Most of the officers didn't like or trust the supervisor, however, senior management loved him. He was always ratting out other officers, even his fellow supervisors. This supervisor had been promoted to a management job in just four years by doing the same thing since he had arrived fresh from the academy.

One day "an anonymous citizen" allegedly called the supervisory officer at the airport. The citizen reported that she had seen one of the Department's enforcement team cars at a Chinese restaurant about 30 miles from the airport at lunch time. The supervisor wrote up a suspension for all four team members, and requested a formal investigation by internal affairs. He never consulted with the supervisor of the enforcement team, or reviewed the Policy and Procedures Manual, which clearly states that when on remote assignment it was acceptable to stop and get lunch— even if you were in a government car. The officers were initially suspended for five days for misusing a government vehicle. The suspension was overturned after a quick investigation revealed the policy manual language and a union grievance was filed.

The internal affairs investigation also revealed that the anonymous phone call originated from the corrupt supervisor's house phone. The miscreant supervisor's wife had deceitfully contrived the false complaint.

- *This supervisor initiated disciplinary action following an "anonymous" complaint even though he knew the source of the allegation was fraudulent. What does this tell us about his ethical barometer?*

- *How would you have responded when you learned that the "anonymous" complaint had originated from the supervisor's home phone?*

- *What, if any, disciplinary action should the supervisor face?*

Oleoresin Capsicum Motivation

A uniformed police officer has been working for a large suburban jurisdiction for about two-years. The officer looks very sharp in uniform, demonstrates an impressive command bearing, and is generally regarding as a solid performer. The rising star is designated as a field training officer, and frequently volunteers to take on the task of taxiing citizen ride-alongs.

The Internal Affairs Division received a complaint from a local attorney who was representing the interest of a client. The attorney tells IA that his client is an undocumented illegal who does not speak any English. The alleged victim was reporting that he had been arrested and injured by the local department. The alleged victim was highly intoxicated at the time of the incident, and as such he could not tell the attorney exactly what had occurred during the arrest. The alleged victim only knew that he may have been at a lock-up of some sort when the incident occurred.

IA investigators interviewed the accused officer. The officer indicated that the arrest was by the book, and vehemently denied that the prisoner had been abused in any way. The officer stated that the only thing unusual at the lock-up was that he (officer) had to drag the prisoner a short distance because the prisoner was too intoxicated to walk.

IA investigators obtained a copy of a videotape that showed the officer/prisoner interaction at the jail. The video showed the handcuffed arrestee literally falling onto the ground as the officer opened the patrol car door. The video also clearly showed the accused officer bending down, shaking his canister of oleo capsicum, and then discharging pepper spray directly into the nostrils of a completely defenseless prisoner. The officer discharged the oleo capsicum into the nostrils of the prisoner a second time before picking the prisoner up and dragging him through the processing bay.

Ranking leaders throughout the chain of command recommended termination and criminal charges against the officer. The Chief of Police however, was most concerned about the impact of the bad publicity upon his legacy. The Chief preferred a private resolution of the incident that would prevent the disgraceful behavior from becoming public. The Chief of Police negotiated a deal that traded prosecution of the officer for a "gag order" settlement with the attorney's from both sides, prohibiting public commentary by anyone involved with the case.

The officer was allowed to resign, and the jurisdiction quietly settled a lawsuit with the victim.

- *Should this law enforcement agency have even entertained a complaint from an undocumented immigrant, who doesn't speak the language, and who candidly admits that he really did not know what happened?*

- *Should the offending officer have been charged with a crime?*

- *Was the Chief of Police right to be "most concerned" about the impact that revealing this horrific violation of trust would have had upon the community?*

- *What, if any, ethical dilemmas are created by the Chief's negotiated "gag order" and concealment of the issue from the public?*

Honest, That Is My Wife's Laptop

While working as the shift supervisor at an airport, a federal police officer turned over a laptop computer to supervision that had been left on the baggage belt at the end of the day after all the flights had been processed. Standard procedure was to open the case, look for identification, and absent any other probable cause for seizure, process it and turn it over to the airline. At that time, the federal agency did not hold leftover property because there were no provisions for lost and found.

As you might expect, the owner of the laptop discovered that his computer was missing when he returned home. The Lojack tracker installed on the laptop broadcast an email to the original owner, who contacted the local police.

Unbeknown to anyone at the time, instead of turning the laptop over to the airline, this supervisor had instead taken the computer to his own home, scrubbed the hard drive and given it to his wife. Police investigation traced the laptop to the federal agency supervisor's home. The laptop was recovered, the supervisor resigned, and the supervisor was arrested for theft.

- ***What impact does weak policy and procedures have upon corruption in the workplace?***

- ***What does the corruption comfort level of this supervisor tell us about his work environment?***

- ***If you were a coworker at this airport, how would you have responded if you had discovered that the supervisor had failed to document and report that a laptop had been found?***

Effect of Morally Bankrupt Toxicity on the Workplace

Dictionary.com. . . defines corrupt as: *guilty of dishonest practices, bribery; lacking integrity; crooked: a corrupt judge. Debased in character; depraved; perverted; wicked; evil.*

The work that follows will help us study some of the more serious consequences of the morally bankrupt manager.

Creates a code of silence work environment: Morally bankrupt managers create a workplace that features cover-ups, denials, and other forms of unscrupulous actions. Dishonorable work environments are erratic and unsafe for employees. Workers cannot count on the organization to do the right thing. Hushed but well known unwritten rules, in place and enforced, permeate the atmosphere making illegitimate customs, mores, and expectations more socially acceptable.

The famed Blue Wall of Silence will not flourish unless an organization has supervisors and administrators who role model, condone, or privately encourage the bad behavior. If those with leadership authority pervert organizational mission, values, and principles, then professionalism in the public service is on a course of eradication. Astonishingly strong individuals can maintain their standards in spite of crooked supervision, but the level of improper behavior is often directly related to the degree of management contamination.

Breeds a law enforcement hypocrite: Few occupations are as preoccupied with integrity, truth, and honesty as public safety. The industry's strong emphasis on principled actions are what makes morally bankrupt bosses so hazardous to its professional health. Law enforcement cultures that feature "the ends justify the means" or "us versus them" protocols cause the ideals and principals of the industry to be in direct conflict with the actions of the practitioners. Hypocritical, deceitful, or immoral law enforcement officers corrode worker integrity and assault the very core of law enforcement's ethical structure.

Morally bankrupt management mutilates the serve and protect model of law enforcement. Compromised individuals can become professionally powerless, even virtual slaves to their illicit masters. Personal reputations and career aspirations are destroyed. Exploitation and perversion also causes business reliability to perish. Corruption of authority by officers leaves residents with the sentiment that they can no longer trust anything that their guardians say or do.

Criminal or civil violations: The damage from millions of dollars in payouts caused by corrupt police activities are self-evident. Facility enhancement, equipment, training, and salary increases are all potential victims of the fallout. Programs get canceled and service levels may change as agencies try to cope with the financial adversity.

The loss of reputation and community trust resulting from the illegal activity of officers is just as dreadful. As shocking as it is, corrupt supervisors are sometimes complicit in direct criminal endeavors such as homicide, rape, burglary, and theft. Lack of oversight and management tolerance are usually major factors when agencies experience scandals involving excessive force, bribery, kickbacks, evidence tampering, protection of illegal activity, or ticket fixing.

Long term consequences: Huge political costs await the law enforcement administration that fails to eliminate morally bankrupt officers from within its ranks. Corruption flourishes in an environment without clear rules and regulation enforcement. We can virtually guarantee changes at the top of the organization when severe criminal and civil violations explode into public view.

Personnel who are immersed in a culture of corruption may find that their allegiance to the institution has declined. Respectable members must ask themselves if this is a department that they want to be a part of. The threat of being branded as a traitor or an outcast is likely to intensify lost time from work. Victims may use absenteeism as a method of seeking relief. Stress, anxiety, sleep disturbance, and depression can all amplify employee medical problems as workers suffer. Turnover is likely to increase as workers flee the misery of tarnished reputations and unhealthy associations.

Corruption of any form has a tendency to be contagious, slippery slope conduct. When a dubious manager has success in the workplace, others are more likely to adopt the same tactics. Morale will be low, and the modeling of bad exploits by supervision increases the chance that employees will institutionalize decadent activities.

15 Ways to Know Toxic Suck-Up Boss When You See One

Sweet, flattering talk to those in authority

Seeks which way the wind blows before making a commitment

Two-faced

Sickeningly agreeable with superior officers

Intently in tune with "what THEY want done"

Accepts and follows orders regardless of their veracity

Insincere both up and down the chain of command

Speaks differently depending on what level they are addressing

Expects employees to do favors for the boss

Overreliance on politics

Closely adheres to policy and procedure

Wants to be around subordinates who are devoted to them

Frequently reminds others of their close relationships with powerful people

False, fake, and living a lie

Tells management exactly what they want to hear

Chapter 12

TOXIC SUCK-UP MANAGER

At first glance, you might suspect that the toxic suck-up manager would be the least threatening of all those that have been previously identified. However, as we shall discover, the long-term danger presented by a suck-up boss is quite poisonous. The most egregious of these managers represent a classic dichotomy in the workplace. Simply put, the toxic a**kisser is loved by the boss, yet despised by everyone else.

The likeability of the artistic suck-up is a mystery to the average worker. Clearly, toxic executives like having the talented suck-up in their inner circle. Many directors actually want to be associated exclusively with people who praise, agree with, and support their every thought and deed. Some administrators seek unchallenged compliance, because in their mind, it verifies and validates that all is well under their watch.

Adulation and excessive flattery successfully feeds the bosses' considerable ego and influences the perception of success. Continuous affirmation of the decisions and actions of the boss can fool the higher-ranking officers into thinking that the suck-up is loyal, safe, and trustworthy. These erroneous perceptions may lead to executives who are hopelessly isolated and out of touch with reality. Impending disaster waits around the corner if the bosses surround themselves with a small group of people who deliver only good news and conceal unappealing information.

The opposing side of the suck-up's relationships also proffers organizational danger. Those that work with or for this type of individual have no trouble seeing through the façade. The constant insincere behavior is obvious and is clearly a blatant attempt try to gain favor with those in power. The groveling, a** kissers themselves may or may not realize that their attempt at personal gain is so transparent. What matters most to the toxic suck-ups is that they obtain the power and influence that goes with cozying up to the person(s) in charge.

One thing is certain, everyday employees understand that their bootlicking co-workers care little about their peers. The brownnosers' focus is solely on what is good for them and their career. Unhealthy competition, mistrust, disrespect, and resentment, are the noxious byproducts of this unwholesome personal agenda. Agency imbalance and blatant favoritism fostered by the success of the suck-up, is likely to cause the wrong people to be put in powerful positions for all the wrong reasons.

The stories that follow are just a few examples of inappropriate conduct by toxic suck-up bosses that far too many of us have witnessed throughout our careers.

Thank You Sir for the Opportunity to Learn so Much from You Tonight, Sir

A mid-size law enforcement agency is involved in working a major ongoing incident—two teens in a canoe on a reservoir in the winter are missing and believed drowned. An extensive search is underway for the boys, involving numerous agencies and countless resources. Chiefs, commanders, officers, and dignitaries of many disciplines have been working on the case for hours.

A law enforcement Major and a Fire Department Battalion Chief are serving as the incident commanders. The law enforcement Major on-duty is relieved for the evening and leaves the command post to go home. As the Major exits and begins walking toward his vehicle, a law enforcement Lieutenant literally bolts from the command post and begins to run after the Major. As he catches up with the Major, the Lieutenant sickeningly says, "Sir, what a pleasure it has been to have worked with you this evening. Sir, I appreciate so very much the opportunity to have learned so much from you tonight sir, thank you sir."

The exchange between the Lieutenant and the Major took place in a parking lot with several public safety witnesses in close proximity. The Lieutenant's tone and voice inflection were overly dramatic and sappy sweet. The on-looking officers and the lower-ranking supervisors who witnessed the Lieutenant's blatant display of boot licking were astonished. As soon as the Major and Lieutenant were out of sight, the witnesses began mocking and belittling the suck-up Lieutenant.

- ***Would your relationship with the Lieutenant have changed if you witnessed his sappy bootlicking toward the Major?***

- ***Did the Lieutenant's groveling and phoniness impact his credibility with his peers?***

- ***If you had witnessed this encounter between the Major and the Lieutenant, what conversation, if any, would you have had with the Lieutenant?***

I've Got It, No I've Got It, No I'll Get It

A large police agency is investigating an abduction case that also involves explosives and threats to blow up numerous buildings. The fugitive is an explosives expert who is believed to be hiding in an apartment complex. A massive search effort is underway for the suspect. Officials from numerous disciplines, including the local Chief and Deputy Chief, are on scene working from a modern command post vehicle.

A Police Major who has a reputation as a "suck-up, yes man" is in the command post. The Major asks the Chiefs if he could do anything to increase their comfort level, and specifically inquires as to their desire for some coffee. The Major happily makes and serves the coffee exactly to the specifications of the Chiefs. Others involved in the situation notice that the Major didn't ask anyone else if he could make them more comfortable.

The Police Department's SWAT team is also on scene involved in the hunt for the suspect. The SWAT team Commander is stationed just outside the command post vehicle. The IC (incident commander) communicates with the SWAT Commander via a sliding window on the side of the command post vehicle.

As the incident evolves, the Deputy Chief of Police wonders out loud about a specific status update regarding the search. When the Chief asked the question, both the aforementioned Major and a Police Captain actually leaped from their seats and hurried toward the SWAT Commander window. The two officials arrived at the window simultaneously and both tried to lean outside in an attempt to be the first to get the answer to the Chief's question. The high-ranking competitors literally *bumped heads*, and both *become temporarily stuck* in the small window opening.

The two high-ranking bosses were so intent on winning favor with the Chief that they made blatant fools of themselves.

- ***Do you think that the behavior of these high ranking officers was viewed positively or negatively by the Chiefs in the Command Post?***

- ***What does the described behavior tell us about the management culture within this department?***

- ***Based on this illustration, are competency and potential for success two of the top criteria for advancement in this agency?***

- ***What are the chances that both of these two competitors receive additional promotions within this agency?***

Yes Sir Captain Sir, I Will Drop Everything to Meet at Your Convenience Sir"

A new police Sergeant is transferred to his second assignment as a supervisor. The Division Commander makes it a point to seek out the new Sergeant on his first day in the office. The commander warmly greets the Sergeant, and states that he would like for the two of them to get together before the day ended to discuss responsibilities and expectations. The commander then asked the Sergeant what time of the day would be best for the meeting.

The Sergeant runs toward the commander and anxiously states "Right now sir, I will drop everything sir, to meet with you at your convenience sir." The commander indicates that it is not necessary to have the conversation at that precise second, and tells the Sergeant to let him know when his schedule is amenable to the meeting. The Sergeant's reply is "Sir, whatever is best for you sir, I would not want to cause any problem sir, sir I am at your service sir." The Sergeant's tone, body language, and voice inflection are distastefully mushy and are interpreted by the commander as a severe case of pandering.

The commander invited the Sergeant inside his closed office for private communication. The commander began to offer some background and perspective on the Sergeant's new assignment and asked the Sergeant to discuss his plans for success in his new job. The Sergeant again makes his remarks with insincere praise of the commander and excessively liberal usage of the word "sir." The Sergeant is so busy sucking-up to the boss that his comments are disjointed and illogical.

The commander decided that it would be helpful to the Sergeant if they spent the next several minutes discussing the difference between polite, respectful conversation and inappropriate praise and sucking-up to those of higher rank. The commander tells the Sergeant that brownnosing is neither desired, nor would it be effective in the current work setting. When asked if he understood the intent of the conversation, the Sergeant said "Yes sir, sir, I'm sorry sir, I didn't intend to offend you sir, I won't do it again sir."

- *How did the Sergeant's initial response to his commander impact the subordinates who witnessed the encounter?*

- *Did this Sergeant's phoniness make him more effective or less effective in his new assignment?*

- *How did the obvious "sucking-up" impact the relationship between the Sergeant and his new commander?*

- ***Do you think that the Sergeant learned the error of his ways and changed his behavior?***

Effect of Toxic Suck-Ups in the Workplace

Dictionary.com . . . *defines ass kissing as: the practice or an instance of attempting to curry favor by the excessive use of compliments, praise, or the like.*

Creates a 3-bags full work environment: The toxic suck-up has only one type of hammer in their toolbox. They spend most of their time repeatedly professing admiration for the manager and praising anything that the boss puts out on the table. Simultaneously, the suck-up will be scanning the work environment for useful worker ideas that they can "borrow" to present up the chain of command. Converting the good ideas of employees into self-righteous proposals furthers the impression that the suck-up is good at coming up with creative concepts.

Insincere admiration and excessive compliments trigger resentment and loss of respect. Due to their political connections, suck-ups often try to influence others by reminding subordinates of their close relations with high-ranking officials. Toxic a** kissing managers are good at stalling, always on the lookout for "how they want it done." Brownnosing bosses continually try to read the tea leaves before making any commitment. "If the boss likes it, I like it," could be the rallying cry of this type of puppet supervisor.

Inconsistent operational priorities – The systematic hazard conveyed by a suck-up boss is pollution that should be avoided like the plague. Incessant, indiscriminate support of the bosses' beliefs and choices subdue member thoughts and inspiration. Toxic "yes" persons accept and follow orders regardless of the legitimacy of the directive. They tend to manage their group by what they feel upper management desires. Flunky supervisors will reverse course several times if they perceive that management has a different thought process in mind.

Groupthink decision-making is a byproduct of toxic pawn guidance. Groupthink by its very nature ignores the fact that there is often more than one way to successfully skin the cat. Overlooking the obvious, and innovation elimination, are just two of the countless drawbacks in ignoring a multifaceted approach to problem-solving. Resolutions to challenges are much more likely to be ordinary, vanilla offerings that are benign and boring. Rigid alignment with the bosses, or betting the farm that the manager is always right, is a strategy that promotes mediocrity or failure.

Blind spot management: Countless agency executives like fawners and flatterers immeasurably, or at the very least, make sure that they occupy positions within their private clique. Supporters who appear to applaud, admire, and back every exploit, feed the ego and validate the self-evaluation of many managers. The grandiose self-image of the executive is fed a steady diet of adulation, verbal stroking, and agreeableness that in due course can change their perceptions of the real world.

The toxic suck-up is using psychological trickery to bamboozle higher-ups. Constant stroking of the ego nourishes a management blind spot that leads to a false sense of favorableness for the wrongdoing suck-up. Many executives feel a sense of comfort when they surround themselves with people whose belief systems are closely aligned with their own. Emotional manipulation; if done well, helps the lesser skilled obtain perks and get promoted to influential positions.

Enduring damage: Toxic suck-ups in the workplace are sowing seeds of deceit that if left untreated can become almost incurable. The overtly false and fake performances of two-faced bosses erode trust, confidence, and crush morale. The insincerity of the suck-up makes dishonesty (both up and down the chain of command) the agencies everyday operational system. The agency itself is contaminated when preferentialism becomes systemic.

Followers do not respect a toxic suck-up manager. When the blatant phoniness leads to success, victims become offended, resentful, and disillusioned. Individuals whose private principles clash with institutional standards will at best be less productive and emotionally detached. Relentless decadent activities by leaders model bad behavior and make it appear to followers that chicanery and overreliance on politics equate to success in the organization. Stress, anxiety, and depression can all amplify employee medical problems as workers agonize over their predicaments.

15 Ways to Know A Toxic Egghead Boss When You See One

Lacks common sense

Overreliance on academic and theoretical concepts

Strong belief that formal education equals superiority

Bolsters their argument by quoting educated people who support their position

Frequently cite educational sources, studies, and stats

Often uncomfortable around people with more talent than credentials

Will use credentials to shut down dissent and win an argument

Lacks flexibility and daring

Focuses on numbers, statistical data, and mathematical validation

Has a hard time relating to ordinary people

Believes that he who goes further in school will go further in life

Low leadership competency

Makes degrees and credentials top priority regarding advancement

Chapter 13

TOXIC EGGHEAD

The discussion that follows about toxic eggheads within the public safety profession is in no-way a condemnation of education. Continuous education and learning enables personal and professional development. Success in the workplace is without a doubt linked to the appropriate and effective application of knowledge and wisdom. I strongly support life-long learning, and encourage all readers to seek understanding while endlessly improving their personal abilities.

The toxic egghead boss in public safety becomes poisonous when there is an overemphasis on diplomas or degrees. Because people possess a higher degree or formal education does not necessarily mean that they will be effective in a public safety job. Credentials can be counterfeit, exaggerated, or immaterial. People regularly pad resumes and even make up certifications. The toxic egghead supervisor; the one who cannot see the forest for the trees, proves repeatedly that credentials by themselves have little or nothing to do with getting the job done successfully.

This problem expresses itself in public safety when leaders confuse credentials and degrees with competency. There can be a big difference between someone who is book smart, or who looks good on paper, and someone who is truly wise and educated. Think for a moment about some of the top performers that you know personally in the public safety business. It is a safe bet that a substantial percentage of the highly skilled go-getters will be known for their experience and common sense, not the possession of academic diplomas.

Problems often arise when toxic egghead bosses are appointed to lead personnel. Egghead bosses usually excel at theoretical concepts and frequently over rely on numerical and statistical data. In the real world of public safety, dealing with people and providing services to the community drives the completion of the mission. Toxic egghead managers may have a gift for mathematical objectives, but they frequently lack the ability to provide strong and effective leadership.

Unmistakably, the combination of academics and hands-on training has fueled professionalism in public safety. Capable employees must demonstrate proficiency with certain skillsets, and certifications help ensure minimal competency. However, intelligence, critical thinking, decision-making ability, work ethic, maturity, wisdom, and personal discipline are but a few of the attributes that cannot be assessed by the accumulation of credentials and degrees.

Public safety is a complex profession that must be driven by competency. Lack of formal education does not mean that someone is incompetent or will fail. Demonstrated ability, not credentialism must be the standard for success. Applicable performance skills that truly make for competence are the great equalizer. Those who do not perform satisfactorily should not remain with the team. Public safety leadership is well served when they focus on demonstrated skills and accomplishments that further the mission of the agency.

The stories that follow are just a few examples of inappropriate conduct by toxic egghead bosses that far too many of us have witnessed throughout our careers.

Dispatch, Send Help Fast

A Lieutenant, an egghead Sergeant, and two officers are on a scene investigating an unexpected natural death of a young adult female. The Lieutenant and the two officers are all physically strong, experienced, highly competent performers. The egghead Sergeant on-scene is a tall, thin, weak, and timid individual whose claim to fame is that he is working on a Doctoral degree.

An emotional family member of the deceased arrived on-scene and attempted to push his way past the officers into the house. When the officers attempt to stop the man, he becomes enraged and aggressive. The family member is a very large man, and due to adrenaline and emotion, he seemed to have superhuman strength. During the physical encounter, the family member is literally pushing multiple officers aside and tossing them around like ragdolls.

The timid egghead Sergeant runs from the outdoor encounter into the house of the deceased. In an abundance of fright, the egghead Sergeant locks himself inside the front door of the residence. The officers who are physically struggling with the family member can see the egghead Sergeant's face in the window as he is peering outside fearfully watching the fracas. The egghead Sergeant picks up his radio and tells dispatchers to "send help fast" because the officers outside are in trouble.

- *Did the egghead officer run into the house and lock the door solely out of fear?*

- *In this situation, physically assisting the other officers never occurred to the egghead. When he thought of helping to resolve the problem, the egghead felt that calling for help from others was the best choice. What does this tell us about the eggheads thought process?*

- *How would you have responded when the egghead Sergeant got on the radio and told dispatch to send help fast?*

- *How would you respond if the egghead Sergeant obtains a promotion shortly after this incident?*

Why Are You Parked in My Spot"

The top 1% of high ranking officials at a public service organization have designated parking spaces near the main entrance to their office building. Parking at this agency is severely restricted and is a significant problem for employees who must come and go from the building during the day. Those who do not have designated parking spots must engage in a parking lot free-for-all that features far fewer spaces than vehicles.

While arriving at the building one day for a staff meeting, a high-level law enforcement manager could not find a place to park. The manager noticed that the #2 ranking administrator's parking spot was unoccupied. Since the administrator was not already in the building, the manager assumed that the underboss was not working for the day. The police manager knowingly parked in the vacant (but designated) spot.

Upon conclusion of the police staff meeting, the manager, attempting to depart, discovered that his vehicle was blocked by another vehicle that was parked in very close proximity. The blocking vehicle, in the travel area of the lot, was perpendicular to the grill of the manager's vehicle as if to form the shape of a letter "T." Travel through the lot was no longer accessible to any other traffic. A note written in red ink had been placed under the windshield of the manager's vehicle, which read, "Why are you parked in my spot? SEE ME" in large letters that conveyed obvious irritation from the author.

The police manager responded to the administrator's office, presented the note and said, "You wanted to speak with me?" The indignant administrator literally throws his keys at the manager and angrily said "Park it! And bring the keys back to me!"

- *What does the ownership of an advantaged parking spot tell us about the philosophy of those who are in charge at this workplace?*

- *How would you have responded when the high ranking administrator threw the keys at you and said park it, and bring the keys back to me?*

- *How would you have responded if you knew that the administrator thought that he was superior to others in his workplace because he possessed an advanced degree?*

Can't See the Forest for the Trees

A highly skilled, well-respected, veteran Sergeant requested permission to attend an advanced driver training course. Upon attainment of certification, the Sergeant was considered the premier driver training instructor for his jurisdiction. The training included execution of a tactic widely known as the "pit maneuver." The low-speed tactic, if properly implemented, is commonly used to control dangerous vehicle situations, protect life and manage civil liability.

The Sergeant and his chain of command prepared a detailed proposal for the Chief and his Commanders regarding implementation of "pit maneuver" training for their entire agency. The proposal included validated nationwide research that supported the technique, case studies, and recommendations of support from the jurisdictional attorneys. Many of those who considered themselves intellectually superior on the Chief's staff personally disagreed with the research and the support from the legal beagles, so they vetoed the proposal and outlawed the technique by implementing a new policy.

More than one-year later, an undercover narcotics detective was involved in a traffic stop of a vehicle suspected of involvement in a drug transaction. It was learned that the detainee was wanted, intoxicated, and likely armed. As the officers re-approached the offender to take him into custody, the suspect fled in his automobile. Officers were pursuing the suspect when he slowed to make a turn onto a ramp leading to a busy Interstate highway.

The driving instructor Sergeant recognized a golden opportunity and utilized the "pit maneuver" to successfully apprehend the offender. No one was hurt, and no uninvolved residents were put in danger. The suspect was arrested, drugs and weapons were recovered, and many potential innocent victims on the highway were spared the danger of a high speed pursuit.

The top officials of this agency were highly upset that the Sergeant had violated the policy that they had created by utilizing a procedure that they had prohibited. The Commanders charged the Sergeant with policy violations and the Chief eventually implemented significant punishment.

- ***Should this Sergeant have "pitted" the violator even though he knew full well that it was a violation of department policy?***

- ***Are you willing to deliberately violate policy when you believe that lives and property can be safeguarded?***

- ***How would you respond if egghead administrators made it clear that they do not agree with a procedure that seemingly saved lives and decreased risks?***

- ***If you were the Sergeant in this case, would you challenge the disciplinary action that was imposed?***

Effect of Toxic Egghead in the Workplace

Dictionary.com . . . defines an egghead as: *A sense of intellectual; highbrow.*

Creates a work environment where credentials over-ride competency: Departments who have toxic eggheads at or near the top of their organization are on a path leading to deep trouble. Once people who are credentialist have power, then everyone who wants to advance within the organization will have to do battle with credentialism. The old saying "birds of a feather flock together" exemplifies the organizational transformation that occurs when the group is led by a toxic egghead executive who believes that credentialism is obviously the best course for all.

The toxic credentialist manager will make significant changes to the personnel policies. The agency begins to make certifications, especially academic degrees, the chief factor in determining hiring or promotion procedures. The result is that many people who could in all likelihood successfully perform public safety jobs are not afforded an opportunity because they fail to meet the new minimum standards. Competency becomes secondary, nothing more than a "nicety if you have it," in the egghead's world.

Interpersonal disconnect: Toxic eggheads place an abnormally high value on the pursuit of formal education. They tend to focus on and follow abstract or philosophical matters. Often the toxic egghead boss is an elitist who thinks that they are superior intellectually. Direct reports usually view them as nerds, or geeks who lack common sense, and who are out-of-touch with ordinary people.

The egghead truly believes that their methods are best for the everyday operational procedures. On the flip side, co-workers feel that the egghead is wasting precious time on imprudent strategies that have no chance of success. The disconnect that exists between these opposite perspectives creates a gap wide enough to drive a tour bus through. Supporters simply cannot effectively follow bosses that are trying to lead them in a direction that the worker instinctively knows will not be successful.

Diminishing quality: Most public safety employees are self-motivated individuals driven by an internal desire to help people and improve the quality of life within the community. When proper funding, equipment, and skills training are added to intrinsic motivation, the results normally are gratifying and relevant. Performance that exceeds the norm is an important value that can be found throughout the public safety business.

When a toxic egghead comes to power, excellence begins to diminish. This is not due to a lack of desire on the part of the egghead. The egghead believes that since they are intellectually superior, the changes they advocate must be best for the organization. Suddenly, outcomes that used to be worthy are no longer good enough. Theory replaces tangible results, and *statistical proof of performance* becomes the prototype that verifies agency success.

Efficiency corrosion causes quality to tumble when bottom-line targets become props for a model designed to make the organization appear to be doing a good job. The working people of the organization know intuitively that the true mission of the agency has been hijacked. The mantra of the talking heads, and the book-keeping of the toxic, makes it look "on-paper" like performance is better than it has ever been. If questioned, the toxic egghead will reply, "I can show stats that prove that our performance is exemplary."

Enduring damage: Toxic egghead managers are sowing seeds of mediocrity in the workplace that if left unchecked will destroy the quality of the organizational work product. The problem for the agency is that the boldness of the toxic professor's self-assurance is not shared by those that he or she is supposed to lead. The result is that the egghead's condescension erodes trust, destroys confidence, and crushes morale. Many toxic eggheads think that the possession of advanced degrees make them the greatest of the great. Those who take direction from the highly credentialed eggheads, realize that a PhD. behind the egghead's name may more closely represent "**P**ile it **H**igher and **D**eeper."

Followers do not have confidence in the toxic egghead. When the overreliance on theories and hypothesis fail to get the job done, it rubs co-workers the wrong way. Annoyance and disenchantment become a part of the daily workplace. If the egghead is allowed to make "working to fill the stat sheet" more important than working to take care of someone in need, then employees will be disconnected, less industrious, and uninspired. Relentless theoretical endeavors by leaders' models bad behavior and makes it appear to followers that abstract schemes and concepts are the most important goals of the organization. Stress, anxiety, and depression can all amplify employee medical problems as workers agonize over their predicaments.

Final Thoughts

Common sense tells us that law enforcement should hire the highest caliber person that they can find. The best individual for the job may or may not be the most educated, or the most experienced applicant in the hiring pool. Top quality talent, once brought on board, can be trained to provide exemplary services. High caliber performers who have proven their merit (perhaps one-to-three years of excellent service) should be encouraged to expand their formal educational level at the department's expense.

A successful employee with a high school diploma could take entry-level college course(s) on company time. Officers who already possessed junior college credits would work towards a Bachelor's degree. Those with a Bachelor's degree will work toward obtaining a graduate degree. The same pattern could also be applied to terminal degrees.

Agencies that choose to invest resources of the magnitude described in the proceeding paragraphs will reap the benefits of what they have sown. The end result will be that the agency has the best of both worlds. Incumbent officers who have already proven their worth in the public safety business, who will, over time, **also** possess the benefits of formal education.

The continuing formal education process will undoubtedly build worker loyalty and commitment. The program as outlined above would guide employees toward a years-of-service mark that makes it highly likely that they will continue on the job. It seems logical that law enforcement agencies would seek to hire the most qualified candidates. The challenge for the profession is to discover which knowledge, skills, and abilities actually identify the applicants who are really the most qualified.

How to Survive the Threat from the Enemy Within

Chapter 14

SURVIVAL TACTICS

All public safety agencies promise to provide a customized version of excellent service to their clients. Energy, focus, and resources ensure that most agencies do a pretty good job of serving and protecting their external constituents. But, what about the internal constituency? The rest of this chapter is dedicated to tactics and techniques intended to help targeted officers stay healthy and survive *the threat from the enemy within.*

Research from around the world tells us that employees do not quit their jobs nearly as much as they flee from their supervisors. As an example, a workplace data analysis firm Evolv – a 2012 study at Xerox (XRX) showed supervisors are the strongest predictor of whether or not employees are going to quit. Overwhelmingly, people change jobs, or change careers because of their boss!

Management toxicity is an institutionalized problem within public safety. A small, but deadly toxic group of law enforcement supervisors create mayhem and leave wreckage within their wake. High turnover, low morale, inefficiency, inexperience, corruption, medical issues, suicide, and homicide are a few of the real life costs associated with poisonous public safety leadership.

In previous chapters, we spent considerable time exploring the identification of toxicity within public safety, common tactics and techniques of toxic bosses, the fact that toxicity is too often a promotional advantage, and the understanding of different types of toxic offenders. Now that we are familiar with the beast before us, let's spend some time discussing proactive options that the targeted officer can consider in response. The ***Toxic Antidotes*** strategies detailed in this chapter include fundamental, concrete and effective techniques that can help the targeted officer survive and even prosper when faced with a toxic threat.

Every situation is unique. There are no magic bullets that automatically guarantee eradication of a toxic cancer. However, the following tactics and techniques have been employed effectively by officers who have found themselves under toxic assault. Note that it is not necessary to deploy the conflict management techniques that follow in a linear order. Much like the use of the force continuum, the *Toxic Antidotes* strategies facilitate flexibility of deployment. Positive results occur when suitable tactics are deployed at an opportune time.

Toxic Antidotes

- Maintain a healthy and balanced lifestyle

- Ensure exceptional performance

- Display strength and confidence

- Create distance between the target and the abuser

- Diffuse and pre-empt challenging situations

- Document, document, document

- Assertively tell the offender the behavior is unwanted and inappropriate

- Master administrative policy and procedure

- Build a support network

- Utilize the appraisal process

- Contact Human Resources

- Explore legal remedies

- Seek alternative employment

Maintain a Healthy and Balanced Lifestyle

An officer who is forced to constantly resist the antagonizing antics of a toxic manager is usually stressed out and frustrated. Continual stress hampers professional achievements, and negatively impacts the balance of a healthy and peaceful existence. Most working people take pride in their accomplishments on the job. The personal onslaught and the implication from a toxic boss that an employee is not up to standard can inflict psychological and physical ailments.

Medical professionals tell us that a proper and healthy lifestyle helps to fight old age, saves on medical bills, reduces stress, and helps build up the immune system. Most know instinctively that exercise, wholesome eating, proper sleep, disease prevention, and a positive state of mind contribute to elite results. A healthy person can enjoy life to the fullest. Equilibrium of perspective and peak physical performance serves as medicinal tonic for those who are seeking relief from toxic behavior.

Ensure Exceptional Performance

When officers are under attack, the best defense lies within the confines of their daily performance. Opinions, attitudes, and methodologies can be debated, but bottom-line outputs are going to be much more difficult to dispute. Good outcomes for the agency and the community provide a layer of rebuttal that could prove to be worth their weight in gold.

Focus on being effective. Good employees ask what they can do to make things better for their organization. Be solution oriented, ensure that workplace concentration is on tasks, projects, and most importantly—results. Update your skills, keep the boss informed (the toxic will reduce performance appraisal ratings if this is not done), and ensure that all reports and documents are completed timely and in accordance with SOP.

Any officer that finds themselves a target of the toxic must do their best work. Exemplary performance can eliminate opportunities that the toxic might use as legitimately destructive ammunition. Improvement and success will boost individual morale, and increased skills will make the employee more valuable to the agency.

Display Strength and Confidence

Displaying strength and confidence is the proverbial double-edged sword when dealing with a toxic boss. In many cases, the target officer has been singled out for abuse precisely because they are viewed as a threat to a weak or insecure manager. However, eye contact, a firm handshake, and a strong confident voice helps an officer project a command bearing that encourages respect from other professionals. In the end, an unfailingly masterful persona will be more difficult for the toxic to undermine.

Officers need to do all that they can to ensure that a toxic boss is not able to derail their career. Regardless of what the officer is experiencing privately, the public image must convey that nothing the toxic abuser says or does will hamper optimism or operational principals. Never let the toxic steal ownership over personal career development and advancement.

Create Distance

An officer's proximity to the toxic boss frequently impacts the depth and frequency of the abuse. Even if the officer is a direct report to the toxic manager, it is wise to limit contact with the offender as much as possible. Lesser exposure provides fewer opportunities to dispense venom. Emotional detachment can also provide a layer of defense. Business compulsion and personal beliefs obligate engagement of duty, but there is no requirement that compels the acceptance of abuse.

Respectfully ignore the toxic boss as much as possible. Restrict the number of one-on-one meetings in private locations. Avoidance techniques such as keeping busy with phone calls, emails, or being legitimately out of the office can also help manage vulnerability. Even in the heat of an offensive moment, consider that it may be perfectly acceptable to simply walk away. Public, stand-up encounters, with witnesses present, increase the likeli-hood of appropriate future behavior from the toxic boss.

Diffuse and Pre-empt Challenging Situations

Everyone shares responsibility for the workplace environ-ment. Though the officer is usually not to blame for the abusive surroundings, there is a duty to avoid escalation and exhaust all reasonable efforts to improve personal domain. Documented at-tempts to deescalate and prevent turmoil are solid evidence for the plaintiff should the situation ever evolve into disciplinary hearings, arbitration, or judicial inquest.

Stay calm, rational, and under control at all times. Angry and nonsensical responses to the pressures of abuse only help the toxic boss trick the officer into making mistakes. Show respect for the supervisor's position, and listen very closely to what is really being said. Pick the situations that are chosen for battle very care-fully. Sometimes the best course of action will be to simply leave it alone. Remember, an officer can be right and still lose the fight.

Learn the toxic boss's tendencies, and identify things that tend to set their emotions ablaze. Anticipate hot button issues and ensure that you have your ducks in a row when those items are part of the discussion. When response is necessary, speak in a profes-sional, yet formal way.

Non-verbal responses may be effective to diffuse some circumstances. Raising an eyebrow, tilting or shaking the head, or a look of disapproval are all actions that clearly convey that the officer does not endorse the offensive behavior. The more talented communicators may be able to deflect or re-direct an encounter with humor. A word to the wise, choose these options very care-fully so as not to exacerbate the tension.

Assertive, intelligent, and befitting verbiage that is well-placed can often change the conversational balance of power. Respectfully asking a supervisor for permission to ask a question is a no-lose proposition for an officer. When an officer says, "Sir, do you mind if I ask a question?" or "Mam, may I offer a different perspective for consideration," the toxic boss will be put in a position where they will most likely answer in the affirmative. The practice of gaining approval for a question appeals to the toxic bosses' sense of superiority, but more importantly, it opens the door so that a sharp officer gains control of the dialog.

Polite statements such as, "Do I understand that you are telling me to …", or "I understood you to say …" are forms of paraphrasing for clarification. Either way that the toxic boss responds will likely prove beneficial to the officer. Probes such as, "What is it that makes you think that …" or, "Exactly what is it that I have said or done that …" are examples of strong clarification statements that should work to the target officer's advantage. Use facts and clarifications versus emotions.

Verbal jousting may or may not turn out to benefit the officer who is battling with the toxic manager. Arguing "yes you did" versus "no, I didn't" offers meager benefits. However, surfacing statements that could later prove to be damaging to a toxic boss, or, making the offender realize the risks associated with their behavior, may very well facilitate reduction of future offensive activity.

Document, Document, Document

Law enforcement officers are keenly aware that prosecution of a criminal case is dependent upon evidence quality. Make no mistake; a successful battle with a toxic boss is also dependent upon the quality of evidence. In any work related dispute, "my word against your word" automatically turns the lower ranking person into the argument loser. Wise officers will use every legal and ethical tool in their toolbox.

The more proof that officers obtain, the more likely they are to prevail. In severe circumstances, an officer must keep a folder or journal of contemporaneous factual incidents with detailed information. Dates, times, witnesses, and exactly "who said and who did what" will prove to be invaluable. Witnesses to an event can be helpful, but witnesses may retreat under pressure, and memories can easily fade. Collect and keep as many hard copies of applicable documents as possible. It is advisable to keep evidence of this kind in a location away from the office.

Advancements in electronics could turn out to be the targeted officer's best friend. Emails and other electronic messages directed to and responses from the target officer will probably be admissible evidence. Electronic questions from the officer to the boss such as, "At our meeting yesterday you told me to ..." or, "I understood your verbal guidance at today's meeting to be ..." clarifies spoken direction and *puts it in writing*. Corroboration of this kind eliminates the "my word against your word" dilemma. Dependent upon privacy rights, electronic messages from third parties may also turn out to be valuable evidence.

Audio and video recordings often prove to be a difference maker during dispute resolution. If it is legal to audiotape or videotape the actions of an abuser, the evidence will be compelling. Officers must ensure that they know and understand applicable state and federal laws that govern overt and surreptitious recordings. Illicit audio recordings are illegal, and most likely will be declared inadmissible and may even be criminally punishable.

Most forms of electronic communications that belong to a government agency are kept on backup files and will normally be retrievable pursuant to state laws and procedures. Much of this information is also available through utilization of the Freedom of Information Act.

Assertively Tell the Toxic Offender the Behavior is Unwanted and Inappropriate

Confrontation with a toxic boss should not be undertaken without considerable contemplation. Every rational employee knows that the power differential between a manager and a lower-ranking worker is fraught with potential danger. From a technical perspective, the boss may hold the power to influence pay, career progression, work assignment, organizational environment, and even the continuation of employment.

With so much at risk, why would an officer even consider confronting a toxic boss? The simple reason is that toxic bosses are unlikely to change without incentive. If an officer finds that they have become the target of vicious personal attacks, then it may be time to firm up the parameters of the relationship. Everyone has their limits, and sometimes the best course of action will be to address the unhealthy activity. The continuation of abominable acts after being warned to 'STOP" becomes very powerful evidence for the aggrieved.

Let's revisit the supervisor - subordinate power differential that I alluded to earlier. It is important to note that the power differential changes altogether when illegal, immoral, or unethical behavior by the boss is involved. The adversary who is morally, ethically and legally right, is the competitor who has genuine power. Unless the system is totally corrupt from top to bottom, it will be extraordinarily difficult for an illicit contention to end up triumphant.

Once an officer makes the decision to challenge the toxic boss, be skillfully firm and tell them in professional terms that personal attacks will not be tolerated. Do not shout, swear, or say things that do not belong in the conversation. Statements such as, "It is not appropriate for me to talk to others this way, and it is not acceptable for you to say … to me either," or "Your screaming, cursing, and threatening makes me feel as though I am in a hostile work environment" are clear, to the point, and easily defensible.

An officer should go into a confrontation with a toxic boss with sufficient armament to emerge triumphant. Point out to the boss with great detail; exactly what actions and behaviors are intolerable. A listing of the grievances may in itself be enough to convince the toxic boss to change course. If necessary, the officer may need to point out the consequences of continuing to push the bad behavior. The officer should not make any threats or issue any challenges that they are not prepared to implement.

Understand that most confrontations with a toxic boss will be unpleasant and not well received. There is a high likelihood that the meeting will curtail the illicit activity, but down the road repercussions are certainly possible and likely. Officers must decide whether or not the circumstances they are facing are significant enough to demand an exercise of the backbone. If the situation is acute or severe enough, then standing up for what is right may be the most prudent action.

Policy and Procedure

Government agencies are terrific at making rules and documenting policies. Nearly all departments have hundreds of pages of written regulations that are intended to govern the actions of their employees. Even though officers commonly detest the huge volumes of jargon, an officer battling with a toxic boss will find golden nuggets within the text. Study applicable policy and procedure as if your professional life depends on the corporate catalog.

Organizational policies on inappropriate behavior and occupational law will almost certainly prohibit the noxious conduct that the officer is experiencing. Hostile and discriminatory working environments are unquestionably against policy, AND contrary to federal law. It is presumable that everything objectionable is prohibited in writing by several different directives. This very fact gives an officer who is following policy to the letter a leg up against an offender when it is time for a third party to investigate and adjudicate allegations.

Build a Support Network

Officers who are enduring toxic managers are under considerable stress. Failure to mitigate the negativity can earnestly impact performance at work and the quality of life at home. Officers should seek relief, and talk to others who can help manage what undeniably is a very unnatural situation. Identify and talk with a mentor, advocate, mature friend, even a counselor who specializes in discriminatory behavior in the workplace. It is probable that others have experienced many of the same predicaments, and wisdom can be found in many arenas.

Use the Appraisal Process

The performance appraisal process is a marvelous forum for addressing concerns and for discussion of new ideas. By design, the appraisal gives an officer an opportunity to inject input, project ideas, address concerns, and talk about things that will enhance his/her chance of future success. The planning for improved performance component of the process unlocks a huge window of opportunity for the astute officer.

Because of the nature of the toxic boss's ego, I am going to suggest that the officer start this discussion with some reward for the supervisor's good behavior. The officer should tell the toxic boss exactly what he or she has done that has turned out to be helpful. The officer may have to reach deep for this, but the payoff could be substantial. Positive statements by the employee about the bosses helpful activity sets the tone for the meeting, encourages continuation of the advantageous behavior, and simultaneously preps the boss for the discussion that is to follow.

When the meeting turns to performance planning, a skilled officer has a chance to address areas of concern with very positive engagement. Statements can be framed so that they do not contain whining or personal attacks. This is a great time to practice the art of "asking permission" to ask a question. Examples of this would be questions such as, "Do you mind if I ask about ..." or "Would it be okay if we have some conversation around the concept of ...." Follow-up to these questions could be in the form of, "Would it be possible for you to ... as this will help me attain our goals," or "It would be helpful if you could ...." The clever officer will prepare these theme questions and concepts well in advance of the appraisal meeting.

Declarative but assertive questions are both tolerable and consequential. If done artfully, an officer has the opportunity to advance concerns, plant the seeds of change, and create expectations all at the same time. When the toxic boss agrees to items that further the officer's future success, the officer has created another layer of ammunition that bolsters their position should the confrontation become formalized.

The appraisal discussion should also include means that highlight the officer's proactive decision making and efficiency improvements. Again, this is documentable evidence that demonstrates that the officer's intentions are to be helpful to the agency and the community.

A final tactic that some officers find helpful involves a request for more autonomy. By asking permission, the officer could say something like, "If you agree, I would like to work the next burglary investigation from start to finish." Upon task completion, the officer should meet with the supervisor to review his or her performance and celebrate prosperity. Building success stories and alleviating management fear provides opportunities to neutralize many toxic bosses.

Contact Human Resources

The dynamics of a trip to the agency HR Directors office make this option one that demands circumspect contemplation. In most cases, targeted officers are desperately seeking relief from what they view as oppression, but we should recognize that often times *others* will see it quite differently. When an officer is facing a situation that is horribly egregious, or if all reasonable efforts have failed to stop the abuse, then it may be time to seek the assistance of a third party outside of the chain of command.

It should be assumed that an employee's trip to HR is a formal complaint that demands investigation. Once that tractor-trailer stars rolling, it is next to impossible to stop it on a dime. When a complaint goes formal, the potential for severe backlash is maximized. Every foray that the toxic boss views as "going over my head" generates controversy, and even minor threats to the kingdom of power could generate ill feelings and attempts to discredit or eliminate the accuser.

When considering the HR option, officers must recognize that no one is going to be cheerful when a complaint is made thru their positional hierarchy. A high-level complaint such as "hostile work environment" triggers inquiry that could affect reputation, veracity, career advancement, compensation, continued employment, violations of law, or even incarceration. Rest assured that the individual, nor the jurisdiction that they represent, will surrender without a fight.

Before going to HR, an officer may wish to consider preparing a well-thought-out written complaint. A verbal complaint will be documented by the HR representative in his or her words. A written complaint should contain all the details and facts verses emotions. This includes documented evidence. It may or may not be necessary to expose all witnesses at this point in time.

Seek Legal Remedy

If an aggrieved officer is contemplating the filing of a formal complaint, it is advisable to seek legal and /or union representation. The manager who is facing serious allegations will almost certainly enjoy the benefit of the agency's attorneys. The job of the jurisdictional attorney is to protect the assets of the government, not the rights of the targeted officer. Since the confrontation will be significant, the officer should look for an attorney who specializes in inappropriate or discriminatory behavior in the workplace.

Use of whistleblower statues will provide some protection for certain challenges. Being the complainant does not make an officer bulletproof, but legal professionals can assist if the officer experiences retribution or retaliation simply because he or she exercised their legal rights. Attorneys may also be useful in helping a targeted officer recover compensation for damages incurred.

Seek Alternative Employment

The bad behavior of a few individuals should not be allowed to force anyone into leaving a job. However, in the worst-case scenarios, walking away from an unhealthy environment is an acceptable option. Individuals must decide for themselves what methodology they will use to regain control of their work life. If resignation is the only viable option, then one must move forward without looking back. No regrets.

Final Thoughts

Everyone has the right to a professional work environment. The obvious question before us is why too many public safety bosses fail to apply the principals of integrity, honor, and courage to the very people with whom they work every day. As discussed throughout this Chapter, how we deal with abuse and degradation will play a huge role in the decimation of the toxic curse. Principled leadership demands that we neutralize the oppressor.

Chapter 15

PRINCIPLED LEADERSHIP

If your actions inspire others to dream more, learn more, do more and become more, you are a leader - John Quincy Adams

This chapter is dedicated to all who are, or have been, fabulous law enforcement leaders. Those who have excelled at leadership have taught valuable lessons, and many of us have learned the trade from some of the nation's finest teachers. These great law enforcement mentors have earned my everlasting respect and gratitude. Paradoxically, we must also tip our hat to the inadvertent tutor, our toxic bosses, who have taught us "what not to do" by modeling bad behavior.

Respectful and artful leadership is the key to undermining or eliminating management toxicity. Masterful leaders who combine expertise, values, and a strong will to do the right thing can become the antonym of the toxic boss. The work that follows in this chapter will help the reader develop a blueprint for leadership success that is applicable to any situation.

As we examine principled leadership, part of our study will be focused on "what great leaders do," in other words, skillful leadership behaviors that are involved with outcomes of excellence. Of equal importance, will be the examination of "who the leader is"; an analysis of convictions, beliefs, traits, and characteristics that explain the intrinsic anatomy of an expert leader.

Lastly, our leadership chapter will focus on the trilogy of principled leadership — 1) exemplary behavior, 2) resolute character, and 3) unyielding courage. Here this loud and clear my friends, principled leaders are obligated to exercise their backbone from time to time. Political favors, conflicts of interest, family members, criminal violations, professional courtesy, and many other predicaments can test a law enforcement leader's mettle. The principled leader's performance must be consistently courageous and ethical in the face of adversity.

Different situations may call for diverse leadership. Good leaders easily adapt the application of various styles and methods to whatever they encounter. There are times when a law enforcement leader must break from conventional wisdom in order to get the job done. In the face of toxic interference, a good leader must often be able to think quickly and impose creative solutions that mitigate the depth of toxic behavior. The illustrations that follow are very different law enforcement situations that highlight principled leadership behavior during real life predicaments. As you peruse the stories, I encourage the reader to contemplate what you might do if faced with similar situations.

Leadership Behavior - <u>Class President</u>

The Chief of a large police agency was an arrogant bully who practiced the policy of favoritism. This Chief also was very well known throughout the region as someone who had a problem with telling the truth. Anyone who had crossed the Chief or who had failed to practice the sheep like behavior of "three bags full," was effectively cut off from the team regardless of rank, skills, or time in grade.

This Chief was committed (at least on paper) to a strong policy of professional development and succession planning for the friendly's on his command staff. The Department practice was to send ranking commanders and those with strong leadership potential to at least one significant national training program annually. The problem was that the Chief and his two Deputy Chief's exercised complete and total control over who was selected to attend. A detailed matrix was used to track which commanders had attended which programs.

A top notch, squared away Lieutenant was working in the Training Division. The Lieutenant, who had demonstrated phenomenal leadership ability throughout his career, was known and respected by people all over the country. Unfortunately, this Lieutenant was in the doghouse with his own department because he was courageous enough to confront the Chief when he caught the Chief in a bold face lie. Though the Lieutenant did not know it, the Chief had been overheard stating that this particular Lieutenant will "never go anywhere or get anything, as long as I am Chief."

The Lieutenant realizes that he had been left out of the professional development cycle ever since he confronted the Chief. The Lieutenant discusses the dilemma with his Captain, indicating that he would like to attend a national program that awards significant college credits for completion. The Captain discusses the matter with his boss, who holds the rank of Major. The Captain and the Major agree that the Lieutenant's skillset is extraordinary. The Captain also gets the Major to agree that the Lieutenant in question had unbelievable leadership potential, and that completion of the top-notch training would benefit the officer, the agency, and the community.

A few weeks later the Captain, without notifying his Major, approved the training request. The Captain and the Lieutenant agreed that the Lieutenant would keep up with the daily activities of his job even though he would be gone for three months out of state. In addition to attending the training program, the Lieutenant maintained his duties at work via email, voicemail, returning of phone messages, etc. and submission of reports. The Lieutenant also returned home on the weekends and caught up on any work necessary for the following week.

While attending the training program, the Lieutenant was honored by 120 of his peers when they elected him Class President. The process of "what you don't know won't hurt you" proceeded peacefully until the head of the nationally known training program sent a letter to the Chief of Police. The executive congratulated the Chief for sending such an exemplary officer to the program. The letter also informed the Chief that his representative had been elected Class President, and invited the Chief to attend the graduation ceremony and bask in the glory of his commander's commencement speech.

The Chief of course, did not know that the Lieutenant he despised was out of town attending the training. The Chief absolutely exploded with anger and demanded to know who had approved the Lieutenant's attendance for the program. The Chief of Police received sheepish 'I don't know anything about this" responses from his Deputy Chief and Major responsible for the Training Division. The Major then called the Training Captain to a meeting to get to the bottom of what he perceived as rogue and disobedient behavior. Since the Chief and the Major both saw the issue as a severe breech of the chain of command, they were determined that heads were going to roll.

When the Major asked the Captain "who approved the Lieutenant for attendance at the program, the Captain replied "you did sir." The Major's face turned white, and he immediately backpedaled and said "I... I... I never approved his attendance." The Captain then refreshed the Major's memory regarding the discussion that the two of them had at a meeting several months back. The Captain reminded the Major that it was "he" who had said that the Lieutenant was a fantastic asset to the department, and it was "he" who had said that the Lieutenant's completion of an advanced program would benefit everyone at the agency and in the community.

The shaken Major just kept repeating "I didn't authorize his attendance." The sharp Captain then congratulated the Major for his insight and decision-making skills regarding his selection. The Captain continued by saying, "After all, the Lieutenant's election as Class President, accompanied by high praise from the Program Director, makes it irrefutably obvious that you made an exceptional choice."

Later that day, the Major limped into the Chief's office and explained that a communication misunderstanding may have allowed the Lieutenant's unauthorized attendance of the program. No further action was taken. The Lieutenant sharpened his skills and was later awarded one of the nation's highest military honors for exceptional leadership in battle.

Leadership Character -
See if the prisoner wants to make a complaint

A well-respected officer is involved in an aggressive physical confrontation with several family members at a domestic violence call. During the confrontation, which included weapons, the officer was literally fighting for his life.

The officer activated the emergency mayday button on his radio. All available officers respond to the location and eventually secured the scene. The officer is injured, his uniform torn and his equipment is damaged. Two bloody combative brothers are taken into custody. One of the prisoners, handcuffed and placed in the police vehicle is screaming, beating his head on the window, and trying to smash the windshield by kicking it.

The on-scene supervisors arrive. The Lieutenant walks over to the Sergeant and says "I want you to go interview the prisoner and see if he wants to make a complaint against the officer." The Sergeant's response to the Lieutenant was, "You have got to be kidding, right?" The Lieutenant indicates that he is not joking, and he forcefully repeats the directive. The stunned Sergeant says to the Lieutenant, "Sir, there is a time and a place for everything; I don't think that it is going to be in anyone's best interest to interview that prisoner right now."

The Lieutenant's face got red, and he aggressively said, "Do as I say, that's an order!" The Sergeant walks over to the police vehicle where the prisoner is located and asks the arresting officer to open the car door. The Sergeant looks at the prisoner, smiles, and says, "Looks like you received an a** whipping today?" The prisoner responds by cursing, threatening, and demeaning the supervisor. The Sergeant then says, "Who do you think might be enjoying your girlfriend while you spend time at the jail?" Again the prisoner responds by cursing, threatening, and demeaning the Sergeant. The Sergeant then asks the prisoner if he had anything else he wanted to say to the supervisor. The prisoner responded by saying, "F #@!!% you! I don't have a f**king thing to say to you!"

The Sergeant walked away and re-engaged in another private conversation with the Lieutenant. The Lieutenant anxiously asks, "What did the prisoner say, does he want to make a complaint on the officer?" The Sergeant tells the Lieutenant, "He said that he didn't have anything to say to me."

Leadership Courage - *Take him out*

A law enforcement leader was serving as the Watch Commander for a large suburban police agency. The Watch Commander in this agency was the highest ranking officer on duty. The Watch Commander from an adjoining large city agency was requesting assistance in the hunt for a killer.

Over a period of approximately 90 minutes, a killer had randomly executed three different victims at three different locations for no apparent reason. The offender was on videotape at two of the crime scenes. The offender's behavior consisted of literally entering a small business, walking up to the cashier, and without provocation shooting the victim in the head. The third related crime was observed by a witness who advised that the victim was also murdered by a stranger without provocation.

The license plate on the suspect's vehicle indicated that he was or had been a resident of the Watch Commander's suburban county. Both police agencies jointly attempted to locate the offender but experienced no immediate success. While utilizing all investigative tools and techniques, the search for the killer continued. Since innocent residents of the city were continuing to be systematically assassinated for no apparent reason, the Watch Commander decided that he should communicate clear and concise directives to County supervisors and officers who may confront the offender.

This Watch Commander met personally with each of the supervisors who were on-duty at the time. After relaying known information, his instructions made it clear that their duty was to safeguard equally both employees and innocent residents. The Watch Commander then issued a directive to "take him out" *preemptively if necessary* to fulfill the obligation of protection of life.

The Watch Commander's authorization of the possibility of a preemptive execution of a suspect was not standard operating procedure in this conservative agency. Detailed conversations about the continuing threat to life, and the dangerousness of the offender ensured that all officers clearly understood the intent of the directive. The supervisors and officers responded with full support for a very unconventional order.

The Watch Commander knew that the fulfillment of his directive would be highly controversial. He was willing to risk personal liability, agency civil liability, legal challenges, moral and ethical predicaments; potential loss of career opportunities, and potential relationship jeopardy with family, friends, and co-workers because he believed that it was the right thing to do under the circumstances.

The DNA of a Principled Leader

Convictions, characteristics, and talent must join with heart and courage to form principled leadership. The composition of leaders and the actions that they take are not complete without the addition of the honorable spirit. The best of the best have that certain something, an intangible moxie, which sets them apart from the norm. The strength of human zest; desire, boldness, and courageousness helps to define the performance of the principled leader. The following bullet points will help us identify the makeup of a principled leader, and help the reader understand what it is that successful leaders actually do.

- *Character / Integrity*

Honest, trustworthy, ethical, respected, worthy, fair, irreproachable, law abiding, upstanding, honorable, factual

Respects human dignity, does the right thing, and speaks the truth. Leads by example, responds in a way that is true to their belief system, and consistently steps in to help when needed. Motivates and encourages associates by modeling professed values. Demonstrates compassion, is the first person in a crowd to rise to a challenge, and performs in an uncorrupted manner even when no one is looking.

- *Exceptional Communicator*

Great listener, eloquent, persuasive, high interpersonal skill, diplomatic, emotional intelligence

Adapts their communication style for the situation, and effectively relates to all audiences. Creates a visceral connection with people by being empathetic, listening intently, responding reflectively, and by thinking before they speak. Asks good questions, uses silence as a tool, and demonstrates that they really care about people in their environment. Inspire others with positive thoughts, and keeps co-workers informed by relaying information appropriately.

- *Authentic*

Genuine, sincere, believable, down to earth, one of us, candid, real, true, straightforward

Leads with the heart, does not seek the limelight, and they desire to make a positive contribution. Statements and actions leave no doubt that they are truly concerned about the welfare of co-workers. Passion is transparent, yet their language is plain-spoken. Consistent realism inspires trust and moves direct reports to followership. Continual self-assessment reinforces the understanding of who they are and what they believe.

- *Mentally Tough*

Iron-willed, rugged, decisive, tenacious, resolute, bold, composed, strong character, emotionally confident

Unfazed when making hard decisions. Digs deep when the going gets tough, strong willed enough to do whatever is equitable regardless of circumstances or consequences. Fortified and committed, they have an unshakeable sense of itinerary, and command. Unwilling to yield to pressure, takes a stand against injustice or inequity even when others may be displeased. Cool-headed decision-maker, confident, and overall soundness. Fierce competitor and formidable opponent.

- *Gutsy*

Risk taker, inner strength, fortitude, confident, tough, bold, brave, fearless, undaunted, stouthearted

Takes smart, measured gambles when they see potential for a huge payoff. Calm and steady during a crisis, makes good decisions on the fly, and relishes rowing against the tide. Says "no" when appropriate, and is willing to wade into danger simply because they see a need that demands action. Slow to retreat, strong, contagious inner confidence instills faith in direct reports. Exudes an aura of daring and conviction that others can see, feel, and almost taste.

- *Good Judgment*

Evaluator, analytical, decipherer, sound decision-maker, reckoning, judging, selection, gauge, estimation, inference

Draws conclusions and makes decisions that are universally viewed as right or correct. Analytical thinker who is skilled at leveraging strength and focus. Triangulates data and frames message so that it resonates with most groups. Able to view components as a whole, but also able to break thoughts down into smaller, more understandable, manageable parts. Right person for the right job at the right time.

- *Diagnostic Skill*

Deduce, assess, appraise, quantify, infer, foresight, intuitive, perceptive, prognostic, insightful, sixth sense

Processes information very quickly and efficiently, can see through the bull while looking directly into the heart of the matter. Formulates alternatives easily, applies deductive reasoning to problems, and expertly ignores confusion and clutter. Able to discern and comprehend the context of an opportunity when examining data. Understands how to prioritize their thoughts and construct a plan of action.

- *Problem Solver*

Solution, fixer, repair, remedy, rectify, correct, unsnarl, adjust, alter, revise, prognostic, convergent thinker

Has a desire to make things right, believes strongly in continual improvement, and is open to change. Superb at weighing options, their minds analyze possibilities in a very organized fashion. Harmonizing a wide array of thought comes easily, they possess a natural desire to make things useful, and they can effortlessly change direction if better information becomes available. Quality analysis of alternatives makes it simple for them to categorize and blend thoughts into a solid plan for improvement.

- *Relationship Builder*

Polite, friendly, humble, interested in others, compassionate, team player, diplomatic, caring, truthful

An outstanding team player and team builder, they talk with people while establishing personal connections. Good one-on-one conversational skills, sincerely inquires into the welfare of their coworkers. They treat people as they would like to be treated, tell the truth, and celebrate the success of peers. They help employees obtain their goals, are empathetic during crisis, and work repetitively to reinforce the positive behaviors that solidify respect and friendship.

- *Coach*

Counselor, teacher, leader, trainer, advisor, questioner, guide, mentor, consultant, tutor

Helps the employee create their own roadmap for success. Encourages the setting of goals and objectives, inspires the person being coached to think and dream big, while ensuring that the student has the tools to be successful. Promotes a lifelong learning mentality in the student that stimulates the quest for improvement.

They look for better ways to perform, and they ask Socratic questions that are designed to lead the learner along the pathway of continuously enhancing performance.

- *Accountable*

Responsible, disciplined, self-watch dog, answer, conscientious, reliable, dependable, fastidious, prudent

Willingly accepts responsibility for choices that they make. When a decision turns out not to be the best option, they will admit mistakes. Understands that due to societal position, they will be scrutinized and held to a higher standard. They do not proliferate blame; in fact they may feel personally responsible when trouble occurs. Exercises strict control over their personal philosophies and activities, and they are ever vigilant while protecting their reputation and legacy.

- *Hard Working*

Industrious, self-motivated, dedicated, dependable, relentless, tireless, energetic, enterprising, dogged, busy

The first to arrive and the last to leave, they will do whatever is necessary to get the job done. Internally driven toward success and accomplishment, they persevere, work long hours, have solid work histories, and do not watch the clock. Positive and intensely focused, they exult in the satisfaction of working, and are motivated by achievements. Astutely understands the connection between hard work, self-direction, empowerment, and fulfillment.

- *Independent*

Autonomous, free spirit, individual, unique, solitary, distinct, straightforward

Enjoys making decisions, figuring out ways to improvise, and the satisfaction that comes from doing it themselves. Courageous enough to stand alone, they are a bit of a rebel, and they do not need a micromanager watching over them to be successful. At ease when left alone at work, most comfortable being an individual who is simultaneously part of the team. May be considered innovative eccentrics who like to do things their way.

- *Self-controlled*

Calm, unruffled, impulse control, self-restraint, even-tempered, level-headed, unflappable, unexcitable, tactful

Keeps temper under control, able to think under pressure, and skillfully makes tough decisions while under duress. Easy going, calm, and composed in crisis mode. Patient, they favorably manage stimuli, impulses, wants, and reactions. If personally attacked, they respond logically, deliberately, and tactfully. Choices most often will be meticulous, logical, and tactically sound.

- *Service Mindset*

Selfless, giving, sacrifice, charitable, benevolent, hospitable, unselfish, role model

Believes that they have a fundamental duty to make the community a better place. Seeks meaningful work, has noble goals, and strongly believes in honor, duty, and the importance of maintaining law and order. Understands the public trust; accepting and relishing the role of protecting the innocent and defenseless against violence and disorder. Willing to work for low pay to help their fellow man because it facilitates a greater good for society.

Final Thoughts

What does your leadership DNA look like? Are you the antithesis of the toxic boss? I encourage you to contemplate the wisdom of the following leadership quotes in the context of the noxious behavior studied in this book. The nationalities, genders, ethnic backgrounds, generational context, and the situational circumstances of our inspirers are wildly diverse, but the wisdom and applicability of their thoughts as they relate to toxic bosses could not be any more on target.

Leadership: The art of getting someone else to do something you want done because he wants to do it.
– Dwight D. Eisenhower

A leader is best when people barely know he exists, when his work is done, his aim fulfilled, they will say: we did it ourselves.
– Lao Tzu

The ultimate measure of a man is not where he stands in moments of comfort, but where he stands at times of challenge and controversy.
– Martin Luther King, Jr.

In matters of style, swim with the current; in matters of principle, stand like a rock.
– Thomas Jefferson

Be the change that you want to see in the world.
– Mahatma Gandhi

A true leader has the confidence to stand alone, the courage to make tough decisions, and the compassion to listen to the needs of others.
– Douglas MacArthur

What you do has far greater impact than what you say.
– Stephen Covey

Never doubt that a small group of thoughtful, concerned citizens can change the world. Indeed it is the only thing that ever has.
– Margaret Mead

Outstanding leaders go out of their way to boost the self-esteem of their personnel.
– Sam Walton

The key to successful leadership today is influence, not authority.
– Kenneth Blanchard

To command is to serve, nothing more and nothing less.
– Andre Malraux

Men are governed only by serving them; the rule is without exception.

– V. Cousin

Good leaders make people feel that they're at the very heart of things, everyone feels that he or she makes a difference to the success of the organization.

– Warren Bennis

People ask the difference between a leader and a boss. The leader works in the open, and the boss in covert.

– Theodore Roosevelt

To be able to lead others, a man must be willing to go forward alone.

– Harry Truman

You can build a throne with bayonets, but you can't sit on it for long.

– Boris Yeltsin

With all due respect to the aforementioned leadership gurus, I paraphrase some of their brilliance to ask, "Where do you stand at times of challenge and controversy?" In the matter of poisonous and toxic bosses, "Are you going to swim with the current, or stand like a rock?" Are you tough, gutsy, and heroic enough to be part of the "small group of thoughtful, concerned citizens" that forges the "changes that they want to see in the world?"

The reactions and practices of the principled leader are unfailingly stable and predictable. Rigid when it comes to their moral paradigms, it is crystal clear to everyone that the principled leader never allows situational ethics to bend the rules or cloud the fulfillment of that which is honorable. Those who are either unwilling or unable to withstand possible repercussions from making hard decisions must find a way to enhance their Deoxyribonucleic acid if they wish to become exemplary leaders.

Chapter 16

CULMINATION – When You Are Right, You Fight

Psychologist and workplace intervention expert, Michelle McQuaid, conducted a recent study of one-thousand people. The study showed bad bosses can cost the economy $360 billion annually in lost productivity. McQuaid says three out of every four people report the most stressful part of their day is dealing with their boss.

Safety is a hallmark of the law enforcement business. Yet, large numbers of public safety officers consistently identify a toxic work environment as their greatest source of stress and threat. Ladies and gentlemen, toxic management is like a cancer, eating away at the integrity of the law enforcement profession. It is long past time to replace the toxic paradigm. All who share a passion for public safety must end their silence. Plato taught us that "We can easily forgive a child who is afraid of the dark; the real tragedy of life is when men are afraid of the light."

Astute leaders guard their name and their word as two of their most important possessions. Reputation, our personal legacy, is a shadow that follows throughout a career and beyond. Much more can be done to ensure that the reflection starring back at us in the mirror is aligned only with the highest caliber professionalism.

Each of us has a duty to marginalize the enemy from within the cherished law enforcement profession. Leadership intervention on this issue is long overdue, and the solution is undeniably straightforward. Consistently rewarding appropriate behavior, and unfailingly punishing toxic behavior, will diminish or eliminate the poison of the toxic practitioner.

Authentic team players look out for the best interest of the agency, coworkers, and the citizens that law enforcement has sworn to serve and protect. Placing oneself on the high ground presents opportunities to prevail and prosper in a less than perfect environment. When faced with agonizing predicaments, rely on conscience and the rumblings of gut instinct. Once an alternative feels right in the heart, and the head, we can trust that we are being guided to a just and ethical decision.

Toxic Boss Blues challenges each person reading this book to stand up to injustice in the workplace. History is full of leaders who rebelled against conventional wisdom because they intuitively understood the need for change. Those who choose to say or do nothing bear the weight of being part of the problem. Leaders who let fear take away their voice should be ashamed. Bravery, fortitude, and courageousness will determine who takes up the crusade against toxic impropriety.

Those who stand up to disreputable exploits are true heroes! Albert Einstein was on target when he said "What is right is not always popular, and what is popular is not always right." Choose your weapons and your battles wisely. When spot-on, stand strong and never give up. A principled leader would rather be hated for what they believe in, than be loved for pretending to be something that they are not.

Doing the right thing regardless of the consequences reveals a leader that everyone can be proud to know! Practice straight talk, never concede one ounce of integrity, and by all means, ***If You're Right You Fight!***

About The Author

Steve Neal served as a law enforcement officer in Virginia for 29 years. During his tenure he was fortunate to experience a wide range of assignments which included Uniform Operations, Criminal Investigations, Covert Operations, Director of the Emergency Communications Center, Director of Training, Support Services Commander, and Inspector for the Office of Professional Standards. He has comprehensive knowledge on the subject of selection and development of a public safety workforce, expertise regarding covert investigations, and a special affinity for media relations.

Steve's distinguished law enforcement career includes many awards and commendations. He is proud of his reputation as a "cop's cop," a leader who places the welfare of those under his command as his top priority. He is respected by those who have served with him, and has been a mentor and coach to many officers. Steve is well known as a man of strong values, straight talk, and true to his word. Rebelling against injustice since childhood, he embodies the doctrine, "When you're right you fight," regardless of political consequences.

Steve was the architect of Public Safety University (PSU), which was a partnership between the public safety community and the University of Richmond. Well over two-hundred officers obtained Bachelor and/or Master degrees through the PSU program.

Co-founder and partner of the Leatherman & Neal public safety consulting team, Steve enjoys providing leadership training for peace officers. In addition to his consultancy, he currently works as a media contributor; furnishing analysis, consultation, and crime commentary for television broadcasters.